Spinning Toward the Sun

*Essays on Writing, Resilience,
& the Creative Life*

benefitting the recovery of Asheville, NC,
after Hurricane Helene

Burlwood Books

Burlwood Books

Austin, Texas
BurlwoodBooks.com

First published in the United States of America
by Burlwood Books 2025

Text copyright © individual authors

Cover design by Andrea Wofford
Back cover art by Kelsey Lecky

Burlwood supports copyright. Copyright promotes diverse voices, sparks creativity, protects free speech, and creates a society that celebrates the arts. Thank you for buying an authorized version and not selling out for a rip-off, and for not trying to make a quick buck by reproducing or distributing any part of this without permission. Practicing common decency helps support writers and, well, just all of us.

ISBN 978-1-961853-07-2

1. Writing 2. Creative Writing 3. Climate Change 4. Community

All rights reserved. No part of this book may be reproduced, stored in a retrieval system, or transmitted in any form, or by any means, electronic, mechanical, photocopying, recording or otherwise, without prior permission of the authors. If you'd like to use some of this book for your class or other fun purpose, just ask! We're pretty nice.

Unless you are using this book to train artificial intelligence (AI). Then our niceness dissipates faster than a poorly-constructed ChatGPT response. Seriously, though -- any, and we mean ANY -- use of any portion of this book, including the cover, to train any form of AI is strictly prohibited. That is copyright infringement. It is not even remotely fair use. And we will seek treble damages for willful infringement plus attorneys fees plus an injunction. You know it's wrong; don't use copyrighted work to train AI.

And now, back to being nice!

To the Asheville community

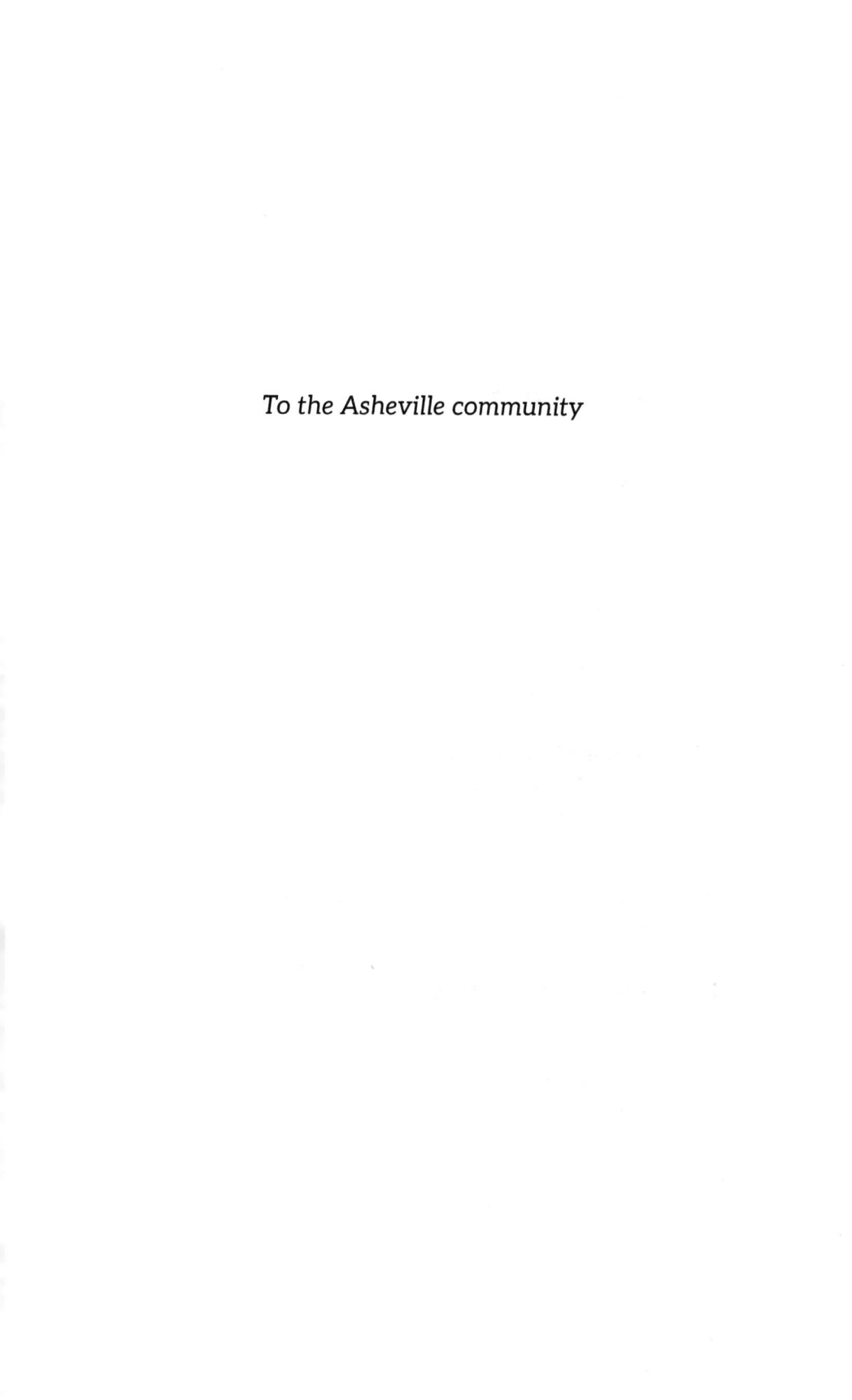

i	INTRODUCTION
1	**In a Flash—Neighbors Helping Neighbors** Amie Darnell Specht (as told to Shannon Hitchcock)
4	**Prophesy & Kinesthesia** William Alexander
7	**The Dictator in My Notebook** Huda Al-Marashi
16	**The Time for Creativity** Sarah Aronson
25	**An Invitation to the Party** Tanya Aydelott
32	**Translating Zappa in Moscow** Linda-Marie Barrett
39	**Remembering Our Worst Times, and Making the Most of Them** Chris Barton
47	**Laughing, Crying, and Barreling Toward Acceptance** Lizzie Brooks
54	**An Antidote to Fear** Nora Shalaway Carpenter
63	**Imposter Syndrome and the Value of the Day Job** Cinda Williams Chima
68	**Hold onto Your (Writer) Friends in Dark Times** Rob Costello

76	**Missed Connections, Misunderstandings, and Misbeliefs: Two Out of Three Ain't Bad, But They Could Be Better**	
	David Macinnis Gill	
88	**Life in Small Doses**	
	Halli Gomez	
92	**Counting Beads**	
	Robin Gow	
96	**Social Thrillers**	
	Alan Gratz	
104	**Room for Purple Horses: An Exploration in Finding Authentic Voice**	
	Lockie Hunter	
109	**Motivation and Swim Buddies**	
	Jennifer Richard Jacobson	
116	**Global Revision**	
	Erin Entrada Kelly	
128	**Shared Light: A Love Letter to Letters**	
	Kelsey Lecky	
135	**My Foot Was Bleeding**	
	Constance Lombardo	
145	**Giving Characters Agency in Restricted Situations**	
	Lyn Miller-Lachmann	
150	**What Climate Fiction Can Teach Us About Hope**	
	Gloria Muñoz	

155	**Look at What I'da Missed**	
	Dr. Chea Parton	
163	**Don't Fear the Spoon: Thoughts on Quitting Your Day Job**	
	Sean Petrie	
182	**Layering in the Details That Matter**	
	Beth Revis	
188	**How I Survive a Monolithic Life**	
	Jess Rinker	
193	**Responding to the Unknown: Creativity as Both Answer and Inspiration**	
	Liz Garton Scanlon	
200	**Living is Creating, Creating is Resiliency**	
	Emma Shalaway	
204	**At the Edge of the Dark, Dark Wood**	
	Megan Shepherd	
209	**What We Carry in Our Guts**	
	Lindsey Stoddard	
215	**Becoming a Writer**	
	Meera Trehan	
220	**Body Language: Acting Out, Scenes Without Obscene Gestures, and Other Effective Ways to Show Emotion**	
	Padma Venkatraman	
224	**Inside Out: Creating Voice Through Building Your Character**	
	Alexandra Villasante	

234 **Sometimes, Ya Gotta Pivot**
Linda Washington

239 **The Five-Minute Talk**
Stacy Wells

243 **Your Voice, Your Story**
Alicia D. Williams

249 **The Writing on the Walls**
Allan Wolf

258 ACKNOWLEDGMENTS

264 ESSAY CREDITS

267 ABOUT THE NONPROFITS

268 ABOUT BURLWOOD

INTRODUCTION

Dear reader:

Thank you. By purchasing this book, you have made a direct contribution to the Hurricane Helene victim recovery. How? 100% of profits from all formats of this book will be split between **Beloved Asheville** and **World Central Kitchen**, two groups who were and continue to be life-saving resources for victims of Helene.

Let me be clear: *No one involved in creating this book—not the publisher nor any of the author-contributors—received any compensation for their time or talent.* We are all donating our work in the hopes that it will inspire readers like you to purchase a copy—as a way both to gain some insight into the craft of writing and the struggles we all share no matter where we live— and perhaps most importantly, to raise more relief funds than most of us could have contributed on our own.

Why these two specific organizations?

Beloved Asheville is a grassroots, equity-focused organization in—you guessed it—Asheville, North Carolina, with an incredible record of service. It was one of the first organizations to get boots on the ground when Hurricane Helene decimated much of Asheville and the surrounding towns.

World Central Kitchen has a similar record of service, although this larger organization is also able to respond to disasters around the world. Just like Beloved Asheville, its recovery aid to Helene victims was almost immediate: by quickly teaming with local volunteer chefs, the organization provided hundreds of thousands of gallons of drinking water and hot, fresh meals to families and individuals in need.

To learn more about these organizations, please visit their websites, www.belovedasheville.com and https://wck.org.

How did this book, a collection of essays about writing and creativity and resilience, come to be?

Asheville is my home. Immediately after Helene hit, so many author friends reached out to see how I was doing (not well) and if my family needed help (we did). Two of those friends—major shout outs to Carrie Ryan and J.P. Davis—even housed my family of five *for multiple weeks* while our power was out, our water undrinkable, and our schools nonoperational. My out-of-area writer friends wanted to help in a meaningful way, but other than donating to relief efforts—I gave them the names of the two organizations above—I told them, rather frustratingly, there really wasn't much they could do.

Then I read one of Rob Costello's blog posts in the free—and oh so excellent—*R(ev)ise and Shine* newsletters. (A version of that post is in this book.) Rob detailed the importance of keeping your writing friends close at all times, but *especially* when things feel truly dire.

I loved that piece. As I was texting Rob to say so, I had a lightbulb moment: maybe there *was* another way my writer friends could help my community. So many of them wrote excellent newsletters and posts like Rob's. So many of them taught craft. So many of them wrote essays about craft, about community, about the resilience of being a writer and a human in difficult times. What a resource that would be, not just for writers, but for anyone who creates! Even better, the book could be a way to raise funds to help the victims struggling around my city and in all the other areas devastated by Helene.

I am what some call a "big picture thinker." In many ways, I operate the oppositive of people like my husband and a number of my dear friends, who relish in minute details and long-term planning. (Opposites, am I right?) In other words, I had a great idea and I had friends eager to help, but I needed someone with actual behind-the-scenes publishing know-how.

As soon as I realized how big of a task this was, I called my good friend Sean Petrie—an author, poet, professor, and owner of Burlwood Books. Burlwood focuses mostly on poetry, so I told him that of course I understood if this project wasn't a good fit, but, "Hey,

Sean, is there any possible chance Burlwood might be interested in not only publishing the book, but...um... not making any money but instead donating all the profit?"

You know the end of the story, of course. You're holding it in your hands. The whole process basically proved the point of Rob's essay. (As I think you'll agree when you read it!) Our community—the relationships we build through real, genuine connection—are our lifelines when tragedy strikes.

And gosh, can it ever strike.

As I write this foreword in February 2025, a mere five years after the COVID pandemic, the United States is in the midst of a fascist takeover, with basic rights being signed away seemingly every new hour; thousands of people remain displaced from Hurricane Helene; thousands more are suffering from wildfires decimating entire communities in Los Angeles. And that's just this week, just in the U.S. The government has now erased the phrase "climate change" from all its websites, as if merely deleting those words could somehow make a global crisis go away. Similar disasters—both natural and manmade—will still happen. (And on a personal note, last month my own world imploded with the sudden loss of my beloved father.)

When I think about all of these events together, it's so incredibly tempting to give in to numbness. To despair. To the horror of so many things beyond my control.

And yet.

Today the frigid February chill gave way to spring-like warmth. Today my children took off their shoes and chased our young dog across a grassy field, shrieking with delight as he outmaneuvered them at every turn. Today I turned my face to the sky and discovered—deep down—that I was still capable of joy.

I thought again of this book, and why I titled it what I did. One of the most prominent memories I have from childhood is spinning—Julie Andrews style—through a hayfield, sun bright and warm on my tipped-up face. Throughout my adult life, I've returned to this memory and the feelings it evokes time and again, partly because of the tangible joy it still triggers deep in my bones. But more and more, I find the image creeping in as a metaphor for not only my writing, but also the very act of existing as a human being in the world.

We're all spinning, all the time.

Some days you wouldn't trade that rush for anything. Some days you'll find yourself disoriented. And some days the dizziness will feel so horrific you think you'll do anything—even give up—to make it stop.

That's where community comes in, offering validation, advice, and support as you regain a sense of equilibrium. These essays remind us all: Keep spinning. Keep writing and creating. Keep reaching out to friends to give and receive help.

Together, no matter how dark it seems, we'll eventually find the sun.

Nora Shalaway Carpenter
Asheville, NC, February 2025

In a Flash—Neighbors Helping Neighbors

AMIE DARNELL SPECHT
(AS TOLD TO SHANNON HITCHCOCK)

We live in the mountains, a place you would never expect to be impacted by a hurricane. Maybe the lesson here is that anything can happen to anybody at any time.

Our ordeal started with so much rain that the creek flooded into the field behind our house.

My husband, Matt, worried our home would lose power. Losing power is a big deal for us because I am wheelchair bound and use an oxygen tank.

On the morning of September 27, 2024, the power went out. Matt switched me to a portable oxygen tank and helped me into my wheelchair. We ate some breakfast and scrolled through our phones, never dreaming of what would happen next.

Bang! We heard a loud noise. Matt checked the basement and water was already halfway up the steps. He packed our medicine, and corralled our pets, knowing we would have to leave everything else behind.

In about fifteen minutes, water rose from the basement onto the first floor. We hurried to the front porch and watched our neighbor, James, wade through waist-deep water, helping others to evacuate.

When it was my turn to be rescued, I was put into a lifejacket, totally dependent on Matt and the other men that live close by. They used my sling (a medical device that makes it easier to lift me), and carried me to a neighbor's house that sits on higher ground. I was drenched and cold.

At our neighbor's house, I lay on the floor in excruciating pain. Water started coming in, and I was lifted onto a couch. The water continued to rise, and I was moved onto a table.

About six hours later, a group of firemen showed up with a canoe and a kayak. I have never been so glad to see help arrive. They placed me into the canoe amid water so deep the men had to swim part of the way.

Thankfully, it only took about five minutes to reach dry land. From there, Matt and I were shuttled in a pickup truck to a fire station, where we spent the night. I can't say we were comfortable, but at least we were together.

I am blessed that my parents live about twenty minutes away, and their house was not in the path of the flash flood. The next morning, Emergency Medical Services (EMS) drove us to their home. Matt and I have been living there ever since.

We lost all the contents of our house, our handicapped-accessible van, my power wheelchair, and so many personal items that are irreplaceable. Some people might not understand, but I lost the ashes of Charlyze, one of my deceased pets. I don't cry much, but that one brought me to tears.

Some of my parents' neighbors have been collecting money to help Matt and me get back into our home. I don't think anybody affected by this hurricane is lucky, but I am thankful that my husband is safe, I am safe, and our pets are safe too.

In the end, our journey is all about the kindness of neighbors and strangers. Without a lot of help, nobody recovers from losing everything. Be good to people and lend a hand, that's what matters most.

Flash flood: A flood caused by heavy or excessive rainfall in a short period of time, generally less than six hours. Flash floods are usually characterized by raging torrents after heavy rains that rip through river beds, urban streets, or mountain canyons sweeping everything before them. They can occur within minutes or a few hours of excessive rainfall. They can also occur even if no rain has fallen, for instance after a levee or dam has failed, or after a sudden release of water by a debris or ice jam. *Source: National Weather Service*

SHANNON HITCHCOCK and AMIE DARNELL SPECHT are co-authors of the middle grade novel, Dancing In The Storm. Their book is a Junior Library Guild Gold Standard Selection and was inspired by Amie's life with Fibrodysplasia Ossificans Progressiva (FOP), one of the rarest genetic disorders in the world.

Prophesy & Kinesthesia

WILLIAM ALEXANDER

First I'm going to share the simplest writing exercise that I know.

Then I'm going to make it complicated.

Here's the exercise: *Describe the thing that you want to write next.*

Before you set out to write the next scene, chapter, short story, picture book, one-act play, or epic novel, spend about ten minutes writing *about* it. Describe it to yourself in a casual, conversational way. This won't be an outline or a summary. It won't look like a project proposal or an elevator pitch. It's just a chat with your notebook. Describe the thing that you want to write next as though you've already read it, and loved it, and kinda remember it.

This simple exercise effectively replaces a messy first draft. Your actual first draft will be more coherent and cohesive, because it will be more familiar. You took the time to remember it before it existed.

Medieval theology described prophesy as remembering. The protagonists of Frank Herbert's *Dune* and Ted Chiang's *Story of Your Life* both remember the future as though it were the past. Writing fiction—and reading it—are also acts of memory. We are capable of remembering things that never happened, and we can try to shape the future accordingly. This rarely goes to plan, though. Mortals make plans to make the gods laugh, and sudden disasters can scramble our whole sense of narrative possibility.

Lots of authors found it strangely difficult to write—or even read—in the early days, weeks, and months of 2020. Pandemic brain brought extra fog to an already opaque and mysterious process. The slow process of creative recovery felt oddly familiar to me; it reminded me of relearning how to walk.

Twenty years ago I went through a bit of spinal surgery, and afterwards my muscle memories no longer applied to the new, titanium-fused way that my skeleton worked. I needed to make new ones. This turned out to be fun.

We usually learn how to walk before learning how to talk, so we rarely remember the experience (because conscious memory is made out of language). The second time I got to pay attention, put it into words, and hold on to the experience. Now, whenever I see toddlers experiment with walking, I can remember what it felt like to build up my own kinesthesia. The synthesis of kinetic proprioperception. The cumulative, sensory understanding of where you are in physical space, where you are going if you happen to be in motion, and how you plan to get there. Gregor Samsa loses kinesthesia in Kafka's *Metamorphosis* because he doesn't know how to move around on so many bug-legs.

Now imagine a kind of narrative kinesthesia—an instinctive, cumulative, kinetic knowledge of story-shape, momentum, and direction. We learned it as children. We absorbed it by listening to picture books and by eavesdropping on grownups whenever they talked about their yesterdays and tomorrows. Language and memory both arrive story-shaped. Once learned, both sorts of kinesthesia become instinctive and easily ignored—unless they disappear.

The best exercise for restoring narrative kinesthesia is to tell yourself a little prophesy. Try it. Avoid formal outlines and hubristic summaries. General Patton famously insisted that plans are worthless—but that planning is essential. This is how we glimpse the untold stories. This is how we remember the future.

Describe the thing that you want to write next.

WILLIAM ALEXANDER *is the author of* <u>Goblin Secrets</u> *and other unrealisms for young readers. His work has won the National Book Award, the Eleanor Cameron Award, the Librarian Favorites Award, the Teacher Favorites Award, and two CBC Best Children's Book of the Year Awards. Sunward, his first novel for grownups, will be published in September of 2025. As a small child he honestly believed that his Cuban family came from the lost island of Atlantis.*

The Dictator in My Notebook

HUDA AL-MARASHI

My mother used to warn me, "Never write anything down you wouldn't want someone to read. Not in a letter. Not in a diary. Once you write something, you can never deny it."

Growing up in Saddam Hussein's Iraq, my mother understood the risks of authorship. Journalists filled prisons and mass graves, and personal writing was no less dangerous. You never knew which of your acquaintances could be an informant, and anything in print carried the possibility of incrimination. And then there was the myriad of social consequences to writing things down. My mother told me many a cautionary tale about girls who had exchanged notes with a boy, or revealed the objects of their affection in a diary, and the family reputations that were subsequently ruined, the future marriage prospects jeopardized.

As a child, I censored my journals. Even though I was born in the United States six years after my parents' immigration, I only allowed myself to write about my school-related stressors: homework, teachers, which of my classmates to honor with the title of best friend. I did not admit to crushes. I did not ruminate on the black spots of sexual abuse in my childhood that I desperately needed to make real.

However, for some reason—perhaps the sheer desperation of needing to confide in someone—this spirit of censorship did not extend to the letters I wrote to Jamila, my only Iraqi-American friend. Our fathers had gone to medical school together in Baghdad, and although our families wound up settling on opposite ends of California, our families were in contact regularly. To her, I would sometimes confess when I'd seen a boy somewhere I deemed cute. She understood the seriousness of these revelations, and this was both a comfort and a bane. I could work myself into a panic, picturing my letters in her house, my name signed to the bottom of such a naughty declaration. I imagined her mother finding my letters, her father, or her brothers. I'd picture my mother being informed of this discovery, her disappointment that I would make such shameless declarations in print.

There must have been something in the act of posting the letter that allowed me to be so brazen. Before I could have a second thought, the envelope would be sealed, a precious stamp affixed to one corner, an investment that could not be wasted. My journals, however, grew so dry and brittle under my self-imposed regulations that I eventually abandoned them. I sometimes dashed off cryptic poems that I stored under my bed, but these were nothing more than bursts of teenage despair. I never thought they could be an indication of literary interest or signs of a future calling.

People like me didn't become writers.

This statement lived in my mind as an incontrovertible truth. It didn't matter if I loved books or if a narrator's voice sometimes lingered inside my head, mimicking what I had just read. Writers were white people with western sounding names who wrote about characters like them, with similar names and lives like the ones I saw in television and movies—nuclear families with homes large enough for one child per bedroom, family dinners at tables set with linens and flatware, men and women who met on their own and dated before they got married.

I didn't read a single Middle Eastern author until college. When I finally discovered Hanan al-Shaykh and Naguib Mahfouz, an entirely new context for my life emerged. Growing up in the United States, I'd believed my household and our traditions would always be mysteries to the dominant culture, so difficult to translate that it was not worth attempting. I accepted that the only time I'd know the relief of seeing the same food and hearing the same dialect was when visiting other Iraqi immigrant families. But these books brought an entirely different legitimacy to my existence. Here were characters in print with names like my relatives, who muttered Quranic verses under their breath for protection, who woke up to recite prayers at dawn, who lived with multiple generations under one roof. Here was proof and confirmation that my classmates could enter this world of prayers and fasting and religious observance through the written word. Here they could empathize. Here they could understand.

Around the same time, I got engaged to my friend Jamila's brother. Although I had planned to pursue an academic career in history after we got married, we wound up moving out of the country. Other moves would follow, and graduate school kept getting postponed.

It was in that void of study that the Twin Towers fell. I wished I belonged to a community of professors and students to process this event that was more than an event but a shift in reality, a shroud burying the life we had known before. Time would not heal this wound. The hate toward Muslims would ripple out for generations. It would ensnare the baby boy I brought into the world exactly one year and two days later in a New York City hospital.

"I am so glad he's fair like you," my husband said, so soon after our son's birth that his age could still be measured in minutes.

"Don't say that," I answered. "He'd be just as beautiful if he got your skin color."

"It's easier this way," he said.

Back at home with our new baby, I didn't know how to make sense of this world—that had turned up the volume on its fear of brown bodies; that whispered of another war in Iraq using mind-boggling claims of its culpability in 9/11; the hate comments I was seeing for the first time on the internet, exposing a level of vitriol towards Muslims I could have never imagined possible.

I turned to books. In that space created by babies and hours planted in a chair breastfeeding, I filled my head with prose. I soon found myself narrating my life as I washed the dishes, swept the floor, and changed the baby. The narrator's voice had returned to the quiet of mind, and with it, the mundane and ordinary transformed into something visible, something meaningful.

I thought of the books I read in college. More than the historical texts, it was the narratives that had stayed with me, the stories that had allowed my classmates to relate to the unfamiliar. I wished I could write something, anything that would make 2003's and then 2004's steadily mounting Iraqi death toll hurt the American psyche more, to render an Iraqi family more human, more than just a headline.

I bought a notebook, my first dedicated to creative writing, but the words spilling out of my pen didn't sound like the words I heard in my head. These were clumsy jumbles, nothing at all like the sure and certain voice in my mind. The physicality of an actual notebook had woken up my censor, reviving my mother's warnings. It wasn't the political dangers of writing holding me back as much as the personal consequences, the shame I imagined I'd bring on my family if I used my life, my stories of growing up as an Iraqi-American, as a window into our world and culture.

I first wrote in pencil, so faint and small you'd have to strain to read, but as the war raged on and the death toll rose, I switched to pen, and then to banging on my keyboard. People were dying every day in Iraq, and the risks to me, for merely writing from my suburban home, were insignificant by comparison. Surely, I could sacrifice my privacy and make my family uncomfortable if it meant that I could make one American reader view Iraqis with more kindness and sympathy.

I had an image of inviting these readers into my family home, that by getting to know me and my parents and grandparents, they'd become our friends and allies. I was so stuck on the idea that I executed it literally. I wrote an entire passage in the second person, taking my audience up the driveway and through the door of my childhood home, sitting them down on the *sufra* laid out on the floor, sharing what we had to eat. I had invited my reader over for dinner.

The writing itself was terrible, the passage soon scrapped, but that exercise did exactly what having people over for dinner does—it created a bond between me and my imaginary readers. It taught me to confide in them, to earn the right to occupy space inside their minds. Every topic that had shamed me before, I now pressed into ink. There was the uncle that molested me. The family friend who arrived a few years later and did the same. There were the first crushes on dreamy Christopher Reeve and the nameless guy from the Preferred Stock cologne ad. There was my engagement to my husband. Our first kiss. Our wedding.

On paper, these memories underwent a transformation, from the private and personal into rough material that I could control. Reveal. Delete. Conceal. Reveal in a different way. There was power in arranging and shaping my experience into stories; in using my life as an entry point not for confession but discussion.

But I would soon realize the power to create art did not transfer into the power to own it. When the first excerpts of my memoir were accepted into anthologies, I struggled to share the news. With the exception of my husband and siblings, no one in my family knew I had been writing. I tried on pen names, various combinations of my first name with Arabic last names, but a fictional name would only undermine what had driven me to memoir in the first place. I was not putting a human face on the Iraqi-American experience if I could not give it my actual face.

Now my censor's purpose was not as much silence but protection from the questions and criticisms that stunt a fragile project's growth. Whenever I shared a publication, I skirted around the question of whether there was a larger work in progress. I needed time to see the merit of a narrative that would find its voice and purpose not over days but over years. I needed time to send my work out in the world and realize that all the catastrophic consequences I had been so certain would befall me never arrived. I needed time to gauge my family's reaction to this role I'd claimed for myself, to recognize that the more I wrote, the less they read and the more normal and ordinary this work became.

Still, when my first book sold, a memoir of my newlywed years, old insecurities rushed to my door, calling out in voices I thought I'd quieted. They warned me of those same dangers of print—now the risk was not a dictatorial regime but these Islamophobic times, now it was the guilt of implicating my entire family in my story-telling, now it was the shame of showing my face at the *masjid* and my children's school with so many details about my personal life swirling around in the vast, unbounded out there.

I fantasized about all the other books I could have written, books full of facts with respectable footnotes and references, books that divulged nothing about me, books that I could discuss with pride. Instead I chose to sit down day after day, year after year, to write about my wedding, my relationship with my spouse, and my struggle for purpose as a twenty-year old bride. Instead I chose to spend years examining my heart, my mind, my small, female life.

I was astounded by my own audacity—who was I to think that I had something worthy of saying, to assume someone somewhere would want to read it? That wasn't who I was in my real life. I was not as bold or as fearless as the words I had written.

My censor had found a new purpose—keeping me from owning my work—but now I knew how to take those same voices that silenced and diminished me back to the page. My writing practice had become my arena to shake off the timeworn, patriarchal stories holding me back, to wrestle with my public and private self, to confront tensions that had no easy fix, no promise of reconciliation, no guarantee of answers.

These days I write less memoir and more children's books. I've learned that if I truly want to combat prejudice, I have to reach people younger and earlier. My censor has also moved on to other concerns. Primarily, why I keep doing this work when my kids are in college and

I have tuition bills that need to be paid and retirement funds that need to be fed. But, lately, it's my mother's warnings of writing's risks that spur me on, that renew my commitment to this work every day. All those years ago, what she was really telling me was not to take the written word lightly. She understood this work has the power to topple dictators. It has gravity; it carries weight.

HUDA AL-MARASHI is the author of the forthcoming middle grade novel <u>Hail Mariam</u> (Kokila) and a coauthor of the middle grade novel <u>Grounded</u> (Abrams), which won the Walter Dean Myers Honor award. She also wrote the memoir <u>First Comes Marriage: My Not-So-Typical American Love Story</u> (Prometheus), which was longlisted for the Chautauqua Prize and a finalist for the Southern California Independent Booksellers' Award. Her other writing has appeared in various anthologies and news outlets, such as the New York Times, Washington Post, LA Times, and al Jazeera. She is a fellow and mentor with the Highlights Foundation Muslim Storytellers Program and a TEDx speaker.

The Time for Creativity

SARAH ARONSON

This week, while visiting a classroom of young writers, a twelve-year-old boy asked, "What do you do when you are stuck? Or can't get started? What do you do when there are a million other things you want to do instead?"

There is a version of this question every time I visit a classroom or lead a retreat with adult writers. How do we stay connected to our stories, especially during challenging times?

Some days, I'm not so sure.

But most days, the trick is separating myself from this complicated, distracting world, which is why I begin my day taking out a pen and drawing swirls. I fill the whole page! This playful exercise by Lynda Barry is meant to help the writer focus on the text and enter what I call the portal of creativity—and the world of the story. Most of the time it works. By the time I'm done drawing, my insecurities and fears have taken a back seat to my imagination and what I want to say.

This act may make creativity sound indulgent—like maybe there are more important things to do. (Well, sometimes, there are.) The truth is, there are times when I feel guilty for spending so much time sitting in my office, looking out at the city of Chicago, and creating something from nothing. Especially when a lot of people are not doing so well. It's easy to turn the page when a disaster isn't happening in front of your eyes.

But then I remember that books—reading them and writing them—is the foundation of so much good. When we write, read, and draw, we are grappling with big ideas. And getting to know people we have met—as well as people we have never met. And we get to explore our obsessions. We ask big questions that our readers can answer. Take it from me, a once reluctant reader who needed a lot of help from an amazing teacher to foster a love of books. (Thanks, Mr. Sigley! I still love *Harriet the Spy*!) When our kids have the freedom to read and write whatever they want, they imagine bigger, better lives for themselves. And that is the first step to solving problems in this very challenging world.

In other words, creativity has never been more essential. It's an important part of repairing the world. From hurricanes. And fires. And the proliferation of fear that manipulates too many people.

Why does this work so well?

When we give people—especially young people—permission to put creativity and curiosity and wonder first, we are giving them permission to explore their own opinions and ideas. We encourage them to reach out of their comfort zones. When we read and write together, we start a conversation. We share our most authentic selves and ask very big questions. We all fail over and over again before we ever get close to succeeding. This is true, no matter what we write or why we write it.

I began my professional writing life twenty-three years ago when someone I barely knew dared me to write.

I took that dare, in part, because I can't say no to a great challenge! Also: I had always loved stories and art, theater, and music. Last: I was curious. I had kept a journal since I was about ten years old. I wondered if I could turn those memories into a story.

One of the first stories I thought about happened between 1972 and 1973. This was the year of big ideas in the world and in my life, thanks to that very encouraging teacher and three important events:

1. I spent much of 1973 living with my family in York, England. During these months, I climbed castles. I read the classics—and then visited the homes of these writers. Met people with different expectations for their futures. I was able to look at and evaluate my home and my life from a distance.
2. I came home empowered. I heard Bella Abzug speak for the first time, which meant it was also the first time I believed that there was a place for a noisy, opinionated, impulsive do-gooder like

me. (I still can't believe I was lucky enough to publish a picture book about her! Young Sarah would not believe it!)
3. I got my first blank book. That book was a gift, and it changed my life. Even before we left for York, I began writing, recording my opinions about everything. When I look at these pages now, I can see the heart of the writer I would become. On these pages are the early words of a girl that felt out of step and slightly different than my peers.

Have you ever felt that way?
Odd? Out of sorts? Like you are on the outside looking in? Like you would never be good enough? Here's a true story. (It's a little embarrassing.)

At first, I wrote nothing.
(I didn't want to wreck my book!)
A few weeks later, I found a project while I was sitting at home feeling sorry for myself: a writing contest. I decided to write a song.

I didn't think music was my medium. I didn't have something burning and important to say. I wrote that song to impress my friends. At that time, I needed something to help me belong. I wanted attention.

I finished my song as fast as I could and put that baby in the mail.

And then, I began bragging about it.
Remember: I really wanted attention!
Back then, bragging was how I masked my fears

and insecurities. At that time, I thought I'd never fit in. As I waited to hear about the contest, I spent a great deal of time practicing my acceptance speech in the mirror. I thought: if I accomplished this, the kids in the neighborhood would like me more.

Well, the letter arrived, and I couldn't believe it! I won second place! I immediately ran outside to brag to my friends and invite them to the awards ceremony.

Can you anticipate what happened next?

Here's a hint: When we write stories, we don't write about perfect people. We write about people who make problems for themselves, who want things that don't come easy, who make mistakes before they grow and change.

Great stories are not about perfect people.

They address our fears. Our wishes. Our yearning.

They are about challenging times.

Well, at the ceremony, I was very excited. I wore a new dress. My mom even let me polish my nails. I sat patiently with my family and friends as the emcee, a man with a lot of hair and a very big voice, announced all the winners as well as how many people entered each contest. That was when we all found out that while there had been many applicants for the fiction, poetry, art, and photography contests, only two people had entered the song contest.

In other words: I lost.

I was too embarrassed to give my speech.

All the way home, my parents tried to downplay what happened. They reminded me that the journey was the point. That I had put myself out there. That was the point. They said they were proud. They put my trophy on the mantel, next to my dad's trophy for being the best professor in the United States.

The funny thing about this story: At the time, these truths sounded hollow, but these are the very same things I now tell other writers. Not only is the process the point. Not only must we write for the love of story. But we must also find ways to validate our efforts—not wait for the stuff we cannot control.

But that is not the reason I'm sharing my embarrassing story here. The point is something bigger. The point has to do with the very mission of writers. And teachers. And libraries.

That night, as we drove home, I realized a bunch of things: First, my imagination was pretty impressive. And my curiosity—well, I didn't need my parents to tell me—that was my super power. And failing? Maybe I didn't appreciate it right away, but these days, I tell readers how important failure and play are to my process, that when I fail, it means I'm reaching. And growing. And changing. Failure is data. It proves I'm making progress—that I care about what I want to say. The effort is worth it. Because books can save lives in a whole bunch of ways:

Books are how we start conversations.

Books are where kids find out that they are not alone. And that there are others going through the same struggles they are.

Stories are how we get to know other people and places, even before we've met them or gone there. Books allow us to travel back in time. And look into the future. Books give readers the chance to feel someone else's emotions. To know what is going on in someone else's heart and head.

But all those things don't make it easy. Well why should it be easy? Stories are important. They are a great way to make the world better like magic. And if the last few years have taught us anything, it's that we could all use a little of that magic.

That's one of the things I love about being a writer.

When I ask readers to tell their peers their truths—the way Bella Abzug did—they share brave and important and inspiring goals. They dream big.

When I invite kids to go ahead and make a Rube Goldberg contraption, they dive right in. There is a lot of laughter and joy—even when the contraptions don't work.

Over the last few years, I have read *Just Like Rube Goldberg* to students all over the world. I have seen what happens when kids are allowed to explore their curiosity, when they are given a voice, when they learn to love learning—for the sake of learning. Not for a test. When they hear a great story, they experience empathy. And joy. And excitement.

They feel hope.

And when we feel hope, we are more likely to face the challenges of the world together.

So, here are some tips that I want to offer you, just in case you are reading this essay, wondering if you should also write a story. Call it my dare, and I hope I hope you will take it.

Get your own blank book. It doesn't have to be fancy. I call mine the curiosity journal and I spend a little time every morning, drawing, writing, and wondering on those pages. (I've got pages of swirls!) That writing sets me up for inspiration. When I am feeling creative, I notice things. I expect inspiration to find me.

And it does.

Listen. Keep your eyes and ears open. Pay attention to the world and the people around you. Engage in deep conversations. Ask questions. When you see someone going through something difficult, instead of judging, ask why. Do not make assumptions.

Have fun. And play. As my first editor told me: Eat dessert first. Forget about perfection! Instead of writing to be famous, write for joy.

Write what excites you.

Write what annoys you.

That goes for reading, too.

This is a promise: creativity leads to more creativity. Curiosity leads to more ideas. And more ideas can lead to compromise, discussion, problem solving, and progress. Can we also promise to stop censoring kids' reading choices? To stop fearing books? Instead, let's fear what life would be like without them.

Here is what I know:

When you read, you are not bored.

When you read, you gain compassion.

When you read, you become a thinker. A leader. A designer. A friend.

And when you write? You lead the way.

In *The Wish List* series, there are three things that every fairy godmother needs to be great. They are three things that I believe we all need to succeed—whatever that means—no matter what you want to do. They are:

Kindness. To others of course. But also, yourself.

Determination—especially in the face of failure.

And gusto.

You know what I think is miraculous? All my characters have gusto—whether they come from my imagination or history. That's why they interest me. Because they overcame failures and went on to do amazing things! And they continue to inspire me as I continue to take chances in this wildly ambitious career we've signed up for.

As for me, I am no longer bragging so much. I love our writing and reading community. I am grateful I have the chance to put my heart on the page and invite others into the conversation.

So now it's your turn.

Open your notebook. Ask yourself:

What's important to you?

What do you have to say?

Who inspires you? How will you make a difference?

Then go out there and do it. We're counting on you.

SARAH ARONSON is the author of books like *The Wish List*, *Just Like Rube Goldberg* (Beach Lane Books), and *Abzuglutely!* (Calkins Creek, an imprint of Astra Books for Young Readers), a picture book about the feminist trailblazer, Bella Abzug. She holds an MFA from Vermont College of Fine Arts and serves as faculty for the Highlights Foundation's Whole Novel Workshops. A former Jewish educator, Sarah continues to join Jewish efforts to combat climate change and take responsibility for repairing the world. Sarah lives in Chicago.

An Invitation to the Party

TANYA AYDELOTT

My mother taught me that a dinner party is successful not merely because of its food, but because of the conversation and company it brings together. Storytelling was a real magic I saw every time my parents invited friends and acquaintances into our home; shared tales and laughter became the means by which they transformed strangers into family. Many of my own narratives draw on in-world storytelling to develop relationships and deepen plots. I think back to my mother's dinner parties and the conversations she so ably guided. What are the connections we forge with each other, and what are the stories that allow us to do so? When magic seems beyond us, how do we call it back through story?

This, to me, is the promise of a good narrative. It is an *invitation*—a chance to seat ourselves at tables groaning under the weight of rich, fragrant foods. Sample this adventure. Taste this fantasy. Sip deeply of this mystery. Partake in the magic of creating something communal, something that encourages recognition. Stories are meant to build us up, to hold us close, to give us the chance to see ourselves as protagonists capable not just of facing difficulty, but of triumphing over challenges. Writing a story—figuring out its burnt edges and sharp flavors, tempering the heat so it can really cook down into its tenderest, most fragrant form—is a *process*, just like devising the menu for a dinner party can be a complicated endeavor. It is a labor, sometimes of love and sometimes of necessity; and sometimes, if everything goes right, we get to welcome new guests to the tables we've just set.

:: ::

Reading came first. Hours spent mapping myself onto protagonists who didn't look like me, but who I wanted to be like. There was Alanna, Tamora Pierce's irrepressible warrior. Harry from Robin McKinley's *The Blue Sword*. Valancy (what a great name!) from L. M. Montgomery's *The Blue Castle*. Louise from Katherine Paterson's *Jacob Have I Loved*, with her awkwardness and too-big hair. Teens trying to fit in or to find their places, to discover their own strengths and the confidence that came from their abilities. Each story gave me a new reassurance that yes, yes, it was absolutely possible to find community and home and comfort. Above all, the books I gravitated toward taught me that a story is a way to create space for yourself.

These are the thoughts I bring with me into my writing projects. I want my stories to feel like meals: to be rich in language and theme, to be heady with unexpected flavors. But I also want them to be places where a reader can find themselves, where they can map their own experiences and understanding of self onto what is happening on the page. This is a kind of magic, separate from the magic of dragons and witches and wondrous fantasy lands, but a magic nonetheless. To be caught up in a story is to be transported.

The thing about fiction is that it is never completely separate from the writer's experience of the world, and it is never completely separate from the readers' experience, either. Some of us wait *years* to feel like a story reflects a part of us that has largely gone ignored in print—either as writers or readers.

But that's the other thing about the fictional table we're setting: it can be big enough for all of us. Being recognized—either in a story you are writing yourself, or unexpectedly in someone else's book—is a gift I hope all of us get to taste and cherish. I can't separate reading from writing, as the one feeds the other. And when I write, now, I think back to one specific moment where a book set the table for me, pulled out a chair, and invited me to feast.

Here's the story of how one single word continues to nourish me.

:: ::

In the house where my mother grew up, shelves are filled with books that open to the right, adorned with words that spill across the page in beautiful, fluid script. Urdu is a language of gorgeous curves, its delicate letters flowing from the right to the left. In speech, Urdu sounds like a quick-moving river: you can hear the current, the wind across the water's surface, the small eddies where the riverbed sinks. It is a language built for poetry.

But I grew up speaking and learning English at an American school in the Middle East. I grew up in the absence of my mother's culture, in a country with a rich and textured history of its own, attending a school that tried to embrace our local community while still holding itself to American school traditions. Summers were spent in either Tennessee, with my father's family, or in Pakistan, with my mother's. The books I had access to weren't about this kind of movement between cultures and countries—and so I had to invent new ways to read myself into the stories I came to love.

When I couldn't find myself in the books in my school library, I began writing myself into the books that were available. I flopped the descriptions of Anne Shirley and Diana Barry in *Anne of Green Gables* so that I might better see myself in the protagonist role. Astrid Lindgren's *Ronia the Robber's Daughter* was a favorite because Ronia was already a punchy brunette. Lessa of Pern? I can't remember how she is actually described by Anne McCaffrey, because in my young mind she looked like me: knobby-kneed, thick-eyebrowed, brown, brown, brown.

I remember reading *In the Year of the Boar and Jackie Robinson* and thinking, "yes, *yes*, I know this"—though, of course, I didn't. I knew a different kind of apart-ness, a different story of being set aside and being lonely in that loneliness. But Bette Bao Lord taught me that my quest to find people like me in books wasn't something I suffered alone; she invited me into a conversation I hadn't realized I needed.

At the same time that I've looked for familiar faces in books, I've been listening in on conversations I cannot join. I hear them when my mother speaks with one of her sisters or a niece on the phone; I listen to the flow and song of her side of their chats and try to find the simple words I recognize. The contexts in which I hear it most have turned Urdu into a language filled with "goodbye" and "I miss you."

A few years ago, I finally recognized my mother's words in a book written for young adults. It's a transliteration, a shifting from the lilt of Urdu script to the flatness of English consonants, but it was on a page, in a book, in my hands. It also wasn't technically Urdu, but this particular word for "goodbye" exists both in my mother's language and in Farsi.

Khodahafes. May God protect you.

I have waited a lifetime to read my mother's words in a book, to hear her voice in the dialogue between characters. *Darius the Great is Not Okay* is not about a Pakistani family. Its protagonist is a teenager whose Iranian mother never taught him Farsi; he is held back from family gatherings, a stranger in a community that should be warm and familiar. Darius is trying to find his place in a world that doesn't hold a place for him, and learning that sometimes the very communities that seem to have kept you out have only been guilty of disguising their welcome.

There is more, of course, and author Adib Khorram offers a complex and nuanced look at multiracial families—transcontinental, transcultural families—and what this can mean for the children who navigate cultures, languages, and loyalties daily in their own homes. I saw so much of my young self in Darius as he struggles between twin feelings: regret that he doesn't know Farsi, and joy that he and his father can bond over *Star Trek*. Does knowing one make up for not knowing the other? Why not?

When I reached the moment in the story that Darius follows his friend Sohrab's example and calls out a farewell to his grandfather—"Khodahafes, Babou"—I had to put down the book. I closed it over my lap as though I were closing one of my grandmother's volumes of Urdu poetry, the back cover facing up so I would open it again to the right.

It is a treasure—a special kind of stirring, wrenching pleasure—to see words on a page that you only remember spoken to acknowledge an absence.

Seeing this word in a published, hardback, *popular* book was something I hadn't realized I needed. I am so happy to be able to gift this book to my nieces and nephews. I want their literary and imagined worlds to be filled with characters who look like them—but also, perhaps more importantly, who speak the words they use at home. I want them to discover pages filled with characters who invite them in with familiar idioms and phrases, even though the words they use may sound like "goodbye."

To see yourself on a page is magic. Hearing your mother tongue spoken by characters you recognize, an unexpected homecoming.

TANYA AYDELOTT is a Pakistani-American author who spent her childhood in the Middle East and Tennessee. She holds an MFA in creative writing for children and young adults from the Vermont College of Fine Arts and is an associate editor for Cast of Wonders, a young adult speculative fiction podcast. Her short fiction has been published in FORESHADOW: Stories to Celebrate the Magic of Reading and Writing YA, Dark Moon Digest, Tales & Feathers Magazine, Podcastle, and Flash Fiction Online. Please visit her online at tanya-aydelott.com

Translating Zappa in Moscow

LINDA-MARIE BARRETT

As I write this, months after the ravages of Hurricane Helene, we are still working to rebuild our community in Asheville. Yet some are working just as hard to tear it apart; people who happen to look or speak differently than me are being rounded up and flown out of our country in a kind of ethnic cleansing. As we witness this situation worsen daily, learning each other's languages and stories—directly connecting through our words— seems more important than ever. For me, that act of creative community is nowhere more vital than in the work of translating.

Most translating, like writing stories, is a solitary art. It is just you and the manuscript, spending countless hours with pencil and paper, grammar books and dictionaries, cross-outs and erasing, patience. You move between complicated, dynamic systems, your brain leaps from one language to the other, persistently hunting for just the right word, and word order, to convey nuance. It's akin to high-level math as you search for the value of the elusive x in the algebraic word problem. You revise and revisit, try to bridge that always-elusive gap between author and reader: Have I captured the spirit of the original? Would a native speaker agree?

By contrast, interpreting is anything but solitary. It is live-action, in-person translating, and can be heaven or hell, depending on your fluency and the subject matter. Technical subjects strain the brain of someone whose training was less practical, more literary. And no matter how much you think you know, you quickly discover the limits of your vocabulary and grammar. I flash back to a Ukrainian stone mason who listened, frowning, as I struggled to explain the dimensions, angles, and materials for a stem wall he was expected to build for one of the church members. The mason and I defaulted to Runglish and hand gestures; we got through it, barely, and I pray the resulting wall was what was hoped for.

My attraction to languages began early. In my tween years, I volunteered summers at a camp for children with special needs. I watched, fascinated, as adults and deaf campers conversed, moving their fingers and lips. I wanted to communicate with the deaf children my age, so I took a course offered by the camp. I can still fingerspell the alphabet, though most signs are long forgotten.

In high school, I took Spanish. In college, I studied Russian, French, and German, one class following another, a quick cup of coffee between breaks to mentally transition between the worlds of da, oui, and ja. When

I first moved to Asheville after graduate school, I interpreted for church-sponsored Ukrainian immigrants. Today I make the most of random opportunities to speak with Russian tourists passing through our city.

Every now and then I pick up one of my books in Russian and open to the pages with turned-down corners. I re-read the comments penciled in the margins during graduate school, where I translated passages into English, or circled a word that didn't have an English counterpart. I was an obsessive translator in those days, feeding a curiosity to make sense of Russian, which to me was like cracking a code to understand the cultural clues signaled by the language. Back then, the Soviet Union was our enemy, but their literature reached deeply into my heart. I wanted to better understand their people on their own terms, through their words.

I faced my biggest challenge doing so in the summer of 1983 when I was in Moscow—and a Soviet pointed a rifle at me and told me to translate Frank Zappa.

I was part of a Russian study group from Colgate University. We spent that summer in Moscow, immersed in Russian classes at the Pushkin Institute. Our dorms were appalling—cockroaches ambled boldly over the toilet and across our bedsheets. Fruit and vegetables were a rarity in the cafeteria. Rumor spread that students who ate meat missed classes due to food poisoning. I subsisted on bread and sweet milky coffee. This was my summer of carbs, weight loss, and cigarettes. A hot, paranoid season in the Soviet Union. The country's leader, Yuri Andropov, was in a coma and dying, our side trip to Kiev was cancelled for security reasons, and the U.S.S.R.

was embroiled in a protracted war in Afghanistan.

Although warned not to befriend Soviets, I was approached by a young Russian, Dima, who became my constant companion. Dima was smart, funny, fairly fluent in English, and desperate to hear about the world outside his country. He was poor, his clothes ill-fitting, his hair shaggy from a self-administered haircut, but he was an intellectual who rose above the indignities life threw at him.

I spent afternoons after my classes walking with him around Moscow. He loved to talk about his country's great writers. He showed me where the novelist Mikhail Bulgakov once lived; he described how the manuscript of *Master and Margarita* was almost lost.

Dima introduced me to his circle of friends. These meetings incurred great risk. Telephones were unplugged when we entered apartments, as this was thought to deter government eavesdropping. At one gathering, Dima brought me into the kitchen to meet the host, where I noticed a man stirring a large pot on the stove. I peered into the pot and asked what he was cooking.

"Poppy pods from Afghanistan," he answered. He was making a form of heroin.

I'll be sent to the Gulag! I thought, horrified. Discovery at this party, however innocent I was of illegal activity, could mean prison. Dima saw I was upset and tried to distract me with a flute—he called me his "Angel with the Flute" and pressed the instrument into my hands—but I shook my head, leaving immediately.

On the night of the Zappa incident, Dima invited me and two of my classmates to his friend's apartment. We drank vodka, passed around a joint (my classmates and I declined, sharing Gulag fears), and discussed pop culture and current events. When the conversation turned to the war in Afghanistan, Dima's friend suddenly became agitated, speaking rapidly. Only two years into our study of Russian, my classmates and I didn't understand much of what he was saying. Our silence seemed to insult him and he left the room.

He came back with a rifle, pointing it at each of us, sneering the word "American." I whispered to Dima that we needed to leave. Dima understood but begged us to stay while he calmed his friend. The friend finally set aside his rifle and put on a Frank Zappa album. Then he motioned to the album and asked me, "What is he saying?"

The rifle was still sitting within his reach. To make things worse, the song was "Bobby Brown (Goes Down)," and I had no idea how to translate the anatomical parts, sexual acts, and slang it referenced. Did this Russian *want* to see me struggle, blushing, not knowing what to do? Or did he really want my help interpreting Zappa's bawdy lyrics?

I didn't have the skill or the presence of mind to do what he was asking. Between the rifle, the joint, and the increasingly uncomfortable vibe, it was time to go. I remember leaving with my friends, Dima and his friend standing in the doorway of the apartment. We were so glad to get out of there that we reached for each other, linking arms and swinging our legs wide as we walked, singing the lyrics to the Monkees' song, "Here We Come."

After the rifle incident, Dima stopped bringing me round to his friends' homes, though we continued to meet on our own and our friendship deepened. He even followed me and my classmates to Leningrad once we'd finished our studies in Moscow. One evening Dima and I failed to get back to my hotel before the bridges went up to allow boats along the canals. We spent the endless white night, the northern sky lit by a soft twilight glow, on an impromptu walking tour of the city's literary landmarks. He kissed me before we parted for the final time. He offered me his heart, which I gently refused. I don't know what has become of him. I hope that he has had a good life, though that sometimes feels like American optimism, not bound by what may have befallen a man like him in a time and place like that.

My summer in the Soviet Union changed me. I now knew what life could be like if we were to lose our freedoms—if life, liberty, and the pursuit of happiness were stripped away from daily existence. I'd experienced firsthand a joyless place with no government accountability, where a candid conversation could mean a trip to jail, or worse. And yet I saw in Dima how we were alike, despite the stark differences in our situations. As we walked together through Moscow, and later Leningrad, we had wonderfully meandering conversations about his world and my world. We spoke in English, we spoke in Russian, and we sometimes didn't speak at all. I believe, in the end, we saw each other truly.

Today we hear local reports of immigrants being tailed, pulled over, harassed, and even taken away by police, of children skipping school because they're afraid to leave their parents, who could be deported without notice. For many the enemy—once the distant Soviet Union—is now right here within our borders, though where you stand on this issue, whom you call the enemy, depends on your politics.

This is where we can do more for our neighbors, to help bridge the language gap between the immigrants who most need our help, and those who most need to understand their stories. Whether translating on-the-spot or over time, learning each other's languages, directly connecting through our words, is more important than ever. It invites a deeper understanding, makes us more empathetic, more able to listen and help, more capable of seeing each other truly.

As we slowly rebuild Asheville, I find myself cracking open the books again and listening to my instructional CDs, rekindling a passion to immerse in a language other than English. But it's not Russian. This time, it's to bring back the Spanish I once spoke so well, to better serve and support our precious community here.

LINDA-MARIE BARRETT is a writer, editor, and the executive director of the Southern Independent Booksellers Alliance (SIBA). She has an MA in Russian Literature and Slavic Linguistics from Cornell University. She edited and contributed to the regional bestselling serial novel Naked Came the Leaf Peeper, *and her translation of "344" by Marina Tsvetaeva was published in the Graham House Review. She writes a blog with her sister, Diane Barrett Tien, Barrett-Sisters.com. Her upcoming book on hosting salons releases in September 2025 with Agate Publishing. She lives with her husband, writer and blogger Jon Mayes, in Asheville, North Carolina. Please visit her at lindamariebarrett.com.*

Remembering Our Worst Times, and Making the Most of Them

CHRIS BARTON

The first time I ever visited the Oklahoma City National Memorial & Museum, I came away in awe of the complex web of tragedy, grief, suffering, heroism, recovery, remembrance, and community spun by the stories it told.

So, of course, I thought, "Picture book!"

Part of that response, I'm sure, stems from the fact that picture books are what I primarily write. As the adage goes, "When all you have is a hammer, everything looks like a nail," and picture books do have a prominent place in my toolbox.

But as I expect will be the case for many who encounter my picture book *All of a Sudden and Forever: Help and Healing After the Oklahoma City Bombing*, the themes explored by the memorial and museum have resonance in lives not directly affected by the tragedy that occurred three decades ago this April.

These lives include those of young readers.

In the story illustrator Nicole Xu and I tell, the details of the terrorist act are not our concern. The text in our book begins:

Sometimes bad things happen, and you have to tell everyone.

Sometimes terrible things happen, and everybody *knows*.

One April morning in 1995, one of those terrible things happened in Oklahoma City. There was a man with a bomb in a big truck.

He parked the truck in front of a big building in the middle of the city. He walked away.

The bomb exploded.

One hundred sixty-eight people died.

The name of that man, let alone his motivation, appears nowhere in the book. This is not his story.

Our focus instead is on how people, individually and as members of a community, respond to great trauma, stress, and pain. On how we recover from and memorialize an awful occurrence. On the ways we remember our worst times—on how we tell and share the stories that emerge—so that we might make the most of them.

While the process we show and describe in this book is specific to Oklahoma City, the emotions involved are universal.

This wasn't the first time I sought to explore those

emotions in a nonfiction book. Years earlier, for a project that never made it past the proposal stage, I wanted to interview Americans who had been children when President Kennedy was assassinated in 1963.

I'd hoped to weave together their personal recollections not only of that dreadful, momentous week, but also of how a new sense of normalcy settled in afterward—a pattern perhaps familiar to those whose childhoods were interrupted by Pearl Harbor, the Space Shuttle *Challenger* explosion, or 9/11. I thought that the perspective gained would be engaging, eye-opening, and instructive for young readers as new terrible events arise.

I also believe such a book would have been helpful to me when I was in third grade and tragedy—on a much more intimate scale—entered my own life with the death of my father.

A carefully written yet honest account of a real tragedy that touched an array of people in different ways over a long period of time, a telling that respected both my intelligence and my youthful sensibilities, and one that gave me a reason for hope—that's a book I would have reached out for.

And that's the sort of book Nicole and I, along with editor Carol Hinz and art director Danielle Carnito, tried to create.

The initial inspiration was spur-of-the-moment—it came with an unplanned tour of the memorial and museum after a school visit in spring 2016—but the writing was gradual, taking shape over the next three years.

After nearly a year of my not doing much more than thinking about this project and discussing it with

Carol, the first version of those opening lines sprang to mind in March 2017.

I began doing database research a couple of days later, organizing my findings by the names of individuals whose stories struck a chord with me. The spreadsheet where I compiled that information ended up with 761 rows. It included at least one row for each person who had died in the bombing and is individually represented in the memorial's Field of Empty Chairs.

For instance, there was a row for victim Carrie Ann Lenz. After the Remembrance Ceremony on the 10th anniversary, an article by John Kifner in *The New York Times* mentioned Lenz, who had been "showing sonogram pictures of her expected baby, five months along, to her colleagues in the Drug Enforcement Administration when the blast struck... The name Michael James Lenz III is also etched on the frosted glass of her chair."

That detail eventually made its way into the text: "Some lost a cousin, a niece, a nephew, an uncle, an aunt, a grandfather, a grandmother, a sister, a brother, a mother, a father, a daughter, a son, a baby named but not yet born." It also inspired my choice to dedicate the book to a child from my first marriage—my son Declan, who was stillborn in 2002.

During a return trip for extended research at the memorial and museum in June 2017, I learned of the substantial efforts to preserve an American elm known as the Survivor Tree so that its genetic offspring (including clones) will remain with us. That's when my focus on the tree began to take shape.

But the book focuses even more on the people affected by the bombing and on their stories, which will endure just as surely as descendants of that elm. That summer I began conducting interviews by phone with survivors, first responders, and members of victims' families.

One morning I realized it was time to start writing, and my first draft—in a voice more measured and less conversational than my default—began to take shape.

While factual, the nonfiction story I found myself crafting was not so much about facts as about feelings. And it was about much more than the Oklahoma City bombing. It was about how people move forward after something devastating, and how people help and connect with each other through new relationships along the way.

For two weeks, I wrote a little bit each morning, working in short bursts so that the intensity of what I was feeling didn't have a chance to fade. I sent a draft of the manuscript to my editor on September 11, 2017.

Events around that time—the attack on protesters of the "Unite the Right" rally in Charlottesville; Hurricanes Harvey, Irma, and Maria; the Las Vegas massacre—gave me occasion after occasion to wonder whether what I had written might be of comfort to a child impacted by the latest public tragedy, or by a private tragedy felt acutely in their own small corner of the world.

Meanwhile, my words continued to gradually take shape. One fall afternoon, the phrase "all of a sudden and forever" occurred to me out of nowhere while I was jogging, and it quickly became our book's title. By

January 2018, Carol and I were talking about the "final polishing" of the manuscript. But we weren't done.

Fifteen months later, she and I—along with Danielle and my wife, Jennifer Ziegler—attended the Remembrance Ceremony on the 24th anniversary of the bombing. We had originally expected the book to be printed by that point, but it was important to all of us that we get this story right, and to gain any insights that might better enable us to do so.

I witnessed, among the reunions taking place, a current of joy I had not anticipated. I welcomed the opportunity to meet some of the people I had interviewed only by phone. And I silently rooted for one of them as she overcame her nervousness and resolutely read aloud her daughter's name and the names of others who had died at that place but whose memories live on.

Soon after, I revised the text for the last time. And with the completion of Nicole's haunting yet accessible artwork, I believed we had created something timeless—though, with its publication occurring just before the declaration of the Covid pandemic, *All of a Sudden and Forever* was perhaps more timely and relevant than any of us would have preferred.

While we don't go into detail about the bombing itself, we extensively address the range of ties severed by the crime, the beloved spaces at least temporarily rendered off limits, the different forms of anguish experienced. Among the people I acknowledge in the text are individuals falsely accused of involvement in the bombing and the parents of those who participated in the plot.

For some readers, these examples will build empathy by providing insight into what those who are suffering may have gone through.

For other readers, our book's matter-of-factness about intense and sometimes confusing emotions will make them feel seen.

For all readers, we show what helpfulness can look like in a dire situation, both for givers of help and for its recipients, whose own opportunities to lend assistance might loom not so far in the future.

As we present in the book, and as many librarians and other educators experienced in assisting young people during difficult times already know, that help often takes the forms of sharing and listening to stories, rather than problem-solving. Our ability to fix things is limited, but our capacity for stories is endless.

And in those stories often reside the common, familiar, healing elements that bind us together in communities. Communities we could not have imagined, and connections to people we would never have expected to encounter. The kinship between those affected by the Oklahoma City bombing and the people they reached out to in the days after 9/11 is an especially striking example and one I'd never heard of before I began my research.

Grief and tragedy know no boundaries and are not reserved for adults. These are difficult, painful, and very real parts of life, even if adults might shy away from addressing them with children.

Getting the words right, saying exactly what needs to be said and in exactly the way it should be expressed, is a tall order. An unreasonable one. In *All of a Sudden and Forever*, my narrator's words falter in one spot and elsewhere are interrupted by a question that will surely be on some readers' minds: "Why?" But each time, those words find their way forward.

Yours can, too.

CHRIS BARTON (www.chrisbarton.info) is the author of picture books including <u>We Match!</u> (2025), bestseller <u>Shark vs. Train</u>, Sibert Honor-winning <u>The Day-Glo Brothers</u>, and <u>Whoosh! Lonnie Johnson's Super-Soaking Stream of Inventions</u>, celebrated on 21 state lists. His newest nonfiction books include <u>Moving Forward</u>, <u>Glitter Everywhere!</u> and <u>How to Make a Book (About My Dog)</u>. Chris and wife Jennifer Ziegler, author of <u>Worser</u>, live in Austin and co-host the children's literature video series *This One's Dedicated to...* He also serves as vice president of the Texas Institute of Letters.

Laughing, Crying, and Barreling Toward Acceptance

LIZZIE BROOKS

In seventh grade I received a trophy for best writer. While other kids were recognized for their prowess on the court or field, I wielded a marble-based genie lamp, supposedly validating my ability to arrange words in a pleasing order.

In high school, I was voted *senior class clown*, arguably a downgrade from my earlier literary accolades. But for me, this title evoked more pride (though maybe not for my parents).

While interests in writing and humor have been center stage since I was young, it's the latter that's kept me from running screaming from the publishing industry.

What's the old saying? *Laughter is the best medicine… for the pain of publishing?*

Ok, I've taken some creative license, but many times upon hearing disappointing book-related news,

I've shaken my head in complete bewilderment and laughed like a madwoman. I've become an expert at scouring shattering situations for comic relief. If not for this skill, a pit of darkness might certainly consume my creative spark.

As far as my online and print magazine publications, I've not had to use my humor–sleuthing skill nearly as much. I've had plenty of rejections, but for the most part, the path to publication in these formats has been relatively smooth.

My traditional picture book journey has been slightly bumpier.

Have you ever seen those death-defying videos of mountain bikers barreling down rocky cliffs? The ones where the helmet cameras shake like maracas and they only get split-second moments of reprieve before being thrust, once again, onto vertical, jerky, potholed trails of hell that signal certain death?

Yes?

Then you have an idea of how my path toward traditional publishing has been.

Stats since 2018:

- Four times in the query trenches
- Eight total agent offers
- Four agents:
    - 1st - a bit too busy with other clients
    - 2nd - dishonest and no longer with the agency
    - 3rd - six-month / single-project agent
    - 4th - my current agent

- 15 times to acquisitions (multiple manuscripts)
- One offer of publication (small, indie press)
- Numerous times "ghosted" after what appeared to be "in the bag"

Looking at this list, it's a wonder I'm still willingly participating in this field. But, as all writers know, the amount of tenacity we either innately have, or develop over time, is colossal. Most of us carry unwavering determination in our bones. We spend months and years bringing thoughts to pen, pen to pages, and pages to gatekeepers who might do one of the following:

1. Ignore the pages
2. Make the pages bleed red with edits
3. Reject the pages
4. Turn the pages into a book
5. Some combination of the above

There are times we might imagine these gatekeepers ripping our pages to shreds, lighting them on fire, and reheating their lattes over them, but it's more likely they're simply reading them and making decisions based on a thousand factors beyond our control.

Some factors beyond our control:

1. The number of titles, themes, and genres of books already selected by the publisher which dictates their list needs
2. The preferences of the editors
3. The preferences of the sales and marketing team

4. The publisher's budget

If our manuscript doesn't fall squarely in the sweet spot of all of these, it gets a pass (regardless of how good it is).

If you're at it long enough, hundreds of rejections will come, as well as the dreaded, *no response,* response. For me, this type is the most painful, especially after being told your work is going to acquisitions. I'm so sorry to anyone who experiences this initial high and eventual devastating low. The lack of closure can leave one's brain properly boggled.

You might ask:

1. Did my manuscript get lost?
2. Did they forget about me?
3. Did the team hate the work so much they can't bring themselves to email a measly, "no thank you?"
4. Did wild animals take over the publisher and because animals can't read, they don't know how to run a press so they can't email me even if they wanted to?

Yes, writer's minds are adept at spinning scenarios (often worst-case), but these tales probably aren't true and acceptances only appear if you continue to submit your work. Sigh...

Back to old sayings: *If you don't laugh, you'll cry.*

While laughter is helpful for coping with these challenging and perplexing upsets, sometimes tears are necessary. Processing the passes with ice cream and an ugly cry has been shown in studies* to increase serotonin and propel authors more resolutely toward their next goal. *All studies referenced were conducted by me (on myself).

On top of laughing and crying, I find there's a powerful third emotional response induced by literary gut-punches: caffeine-fueled rants about the brokenness of the business. I suggest indulging in these with your writer friends as they truly understand the subjective, grueling, and devastating aspects you'll snarl on about.

Of course, share your feelings with your non-writer friends and family as well, but don't expect the same level of understanding. They *want* to understand, but realistically, that level of empathy only develops after years of being steeped in the boiling waters of the book biz.

Other things only your writer friends will understand:

1. The mortifying moment when you hit send on a query and realize you misspelled the agent's or editor's name—or worse yet—addressed it to a different person entirely.
2. Feeling like you've written the best thing you'll ever write only to have your critique partners tell you it's trash (they won't call it *trash*, but that will be your interpretation).
3. Writing what you think is trash only to have your critique partners tell you it's the best thing you've ever written (then feeling paralyzed about

where to go from there).
4. Getting a rejection within five minutes of submitting.
5. Getting a rejection after over a year on submission.
6. Coming up with a brilliant idea, Googling it, and realizing it already exists.

If/when any of these things occur, just know they're rites of passage. Take a deep breath and however much you want to, don't throw your computer in a lake. Keep believing the work into being and, one day, it will be bound and at your fingertips.

I've heard writers say that they hold "blind faith" to continue in this industry. They believe that if they maintain hope, their work will be read, accepted, shared, and cherished. And while this is valid, I'd argue that what we call "blind" isn't actually blind at all.

Blind faith is defined as *the act of believing something without a reasonable basis/believing something even when it's unreasonable or wrong.*

But with our work, we *know* the material we have faith in. We're not blind to the characters, themes, settings, plots, and emotional arcs that our word-weaving created. We know the countless iterations, changes in POV, tense, and tone that we've worked tirelessly to create.

All this is to say that our faith is nowhere near *blind*—it's knowledge-based. Humility has its place, but so does the honest-to-goodness truth that the work is *good* and deserves to be published. It may seem harsh, but no one will care more about your writing than you do.

So, be a cheerleader for your work and the work of others. Do literary backflips by diving into new ideas and revisions, spending time critiquing others' work, reading extensively, leaving honest reviews, and sharing your love of books. Shake your head and your pom-poms at rejections and stand on the shoulders of the literary giants who came before to inspire your path.

If you stick it out, who knows?

You might get a trophy.

LIZZIE BROOKS is a mom, yoga teacher, and writer whose work is published with Yoga International, Door = Jar Literary Magazine, Beyond Words Literary, and more. Her children's work is represented by Jen Newens of Martin Literary. She runs a mom & pop style critique and pitch-writing business that allows her to support writers in their journey toward publication. She lives in the mountains with her husband, son, and two dogs—none of whom enjoy her constant puns as much as she does. Find her at www.lizziebrooksbooks.net

An Antidote to Fear

NORA SHALAWAY CARPENTER

It took me years to work up the courage to write my newest novel, *Fault Lines*, which has fracking and socioeconomic disparity at the heart of its plot. Partly that was because younger Nora recognized I needed to become a stronger writer to produce the complex emotional core the story demanded. But mostly I was afraid of how the story I felt deeply called to tell might alienate me from people I care about, namely members of the community in which I grew up in rural West Virginia. A community that has always relied heavily on environmental extraction.

A deeper part of me knew I was also fearful because I had to lean into, research, and even—for one of the two point-of-view characters—write from the perspective of a teenager whose worldview and values not only differed from my own; they underscored environmental practices that did real world damage. And for context, I'm the daughter of a wildlife biologist, so care for the environment was fundamental to my upbringing.

My fears morphed and extended so much that sometimes I wondered if I was capable of doing the story justice. More than once I feared that by highlighting the nuances of an issue that people loved to paint in stark strokes of black and white, maybe I'd just alienate everyone—environmentalists and energy extractors alike. Sometimes I had so much fear about this, it was difficult to write at all.

And yet, the story would not let me be.

It was community that saved me. Community comprised of others doing the same, complex work and coming together to share ideas, frustrations, encouragement, and innovations. For me, I turned to my author friends, fellow artists who understood the pressure of writing during the age of massive book bans. *What if the book gets banned?* I worried. *What if I get cancelled? What if the entire point of the story is missed because it disrupts the easy, righteous narrative in which adult gatekeepers feel comfortable.*

What if? What if? WHAT IF?

I talked to a lot of writers, but my AHA! moment came during a conversation several years ago with author Crystal Allen, a trusted friend and fellow *Highlights* faculty member. After listening to my concerns—my *fears*—she gave me advice I will never forget. Advice I return to again and again.

"The way I see it is this," she told me. (I'm paraphrasing but this is the gist.) "It's a creator's job to ask the hard questions. To reveal difficult truths even when that means taking creative risks and possibly making people, friends even, uncomfortable. To push people outside of their comfort zones, if that's what it takes to find a little bit more of the truth. How else can we make anything that matters?"

I felt the truth of what she said tangibly, in my gut. In that moment, Crystal gave fearful Nora what she needed the most: permission and power. She didn't take away the fear, but she helped me remember that what I was trying to do was worth my—and others'—discomfort. Put another way, Crystal's words enabled my words, so that my words could reach the readers who needed them. **That's what community does.**

I'm telling you this story because there is a lot of fear in the air right now. Fear over election results, and rampant ecological disasters. And while it is most certainly a valid emotion and should be honored instead of repressed, fear should never be allowed to lead. Fear is the antithesis of hope. It's the antithesis of humanity. Fear will try its darndest to squash our dreams.

If I had let fear guide me, *Fault Lines* would be a different book. Maybe the novel that ended up garnering my first big monetary award—the Green Earth Book Award—wouldn't exist at all. But thanks to my community of fellow authors, particularly Crystal, I found the courage to write the truth as I saw it. To tell the intertwined stories of two very different teenagers whose life experiences lead them to believe very different things, but who nonetheless discover that each of them just might be exactly the person the other needs to heal and grow at this point in their life.

Fault Lines doesn't offer easy or pedantic solutions, but I do hope it makes every reader imagine the possibilities that might exist if more people like Viv and Dex were able to come together.

What kind of world could we live in—what kind of progress could we make—if we actually *listened* to each other before presenting our own arguments? If we put our self-righteousness (we all have some form of it) on hold and acknowledged *what we don't know about experiences we've never had and listen to people who've had them.* If we allowed our minds to grow, our ideas to re-route and re-root? If we used our differences to discover solutions that might not have been possible if we hadn't challenged each other through honest, respectful debate?

Interestingly, right before the 2024 election, I learned that one of my books *is* banned, though it's not *Fault Lines*. My first anthology, *Rural Voices: 15 Authors Challenge Stereotypes About Small-Town America* is now banned in several districts in Georgia and Florida.

And of course many of my fellow authors have multiple of their books banned, and there is proposed legislation that seriously threatens creators and educators. Legislation that is, to me, quite frankly, terrifying.

But that's the point, isn't it? The goal of fear is to scare us into silence, and to perpetuate the myth that we need to be afraid of one another. Fear wants to separate us. To force us out of community and into isolation. Because the whole point of *Rural Voices* is to show the world that rural teens have the same hopes, dreams, worries, sacrifices, talents, and humanity as any other teenager. And I will never stop advocating that fact.

Now at this point I want to be very clear: because of our color, personal traumas, experiences, and where we live, we cannot all resist in the same way. A lot of students are probably worrying about getting their basic needs met, and perhaps educators are, too. Perhaps you too are wondering, *How can I do the work of my heart and still keep my job?*

At times like this, it can be tempting—so very, very tempting—to give up. To let the hugeness of fear swallow us whole, engulfing both our spirit and our voice.

We don't have an easy road ahead of us, but history has shown us that the antidote to fear and oppression is community. Making connections with others so that you can discover all the work being done and how you can fit into it while still ensuring your personal safety. Community also allows those of us who are able to take more risks to step up and do so, while those who can't can offer support in other ways.

Community is where we can rediscover the heart, hope, and humanity of the world, even—and especially—when we are at our deepest points of despair.

I urge you ... seek out and meet new people. Attend a conference and step outside your comfort zone by introducing yourself to someone. Sit at a table of strangers and connect. Exchange emails, phone numbers, ideas. Build your own smaller communities that can address your most important shared needs. Communities that you can rely on again and again as we choose every day to work in pursuit of truth.

Because while giving up might feel like the only

option sometimes, and speaking your truth might make you less popular in some circles, those of us who teach and write for children and young adults cannot abandon the very people who need us the most—kids—in a time when they are most in need. Our students, our readers, are watching us. How are we reacting? Are we spewing hate back at those being hateful and giving in to fear? Or are we channeling our rage, despair, and other huge emotions into building a protective community of resistance?

For those of you who are rural educators, or who care deeply about rural students, perhaps the most important thing you can do for your students is empower them to build their own life-saving communities. I am continually heartened and inspired by the number of incredible rural-focused organizations that exist today, including Rural Minds, Literacy in Place, the Rural Library Network, the Daily Yonder, and the Rural Impact podcast, among others.

Part of helping rural students is by sharing resources like these, many of which have podcasts and social media that appeals to teens. Please check them out. You can find more on the Rural Resources page of my website, noracarpenterwrites.com, which I'm continually updating.

At this point, some of you may be thinking, "What about my students who aren't feeling fear right now, but joy? Who truly believe the next administration is going to serve their interests?" Perhaps you teach students who espouse the bigoted and hate-filled ideas that terrify some of their classmates.

I grew up in classrooms like this, and I know how many of them still exist today.

The answer I offer again is community.

Some of your students will need additional smaller communities to feel safe, but we can't neglect the importance of classroom community, comprised as it will be with varying beliefs, some of which will be fundamentally opposed to yours. But we cannot isolate, as fear would have us do. Few minds are changed by yelling and fact throwing. Minds are changed by hearts. And hearts are changed by community. And community is established by sharing stories.

I want to share some brain science that Lisa Cron explains in her remarkable craft guide, *Story Genius*: "Functional MRI studies reveal that when we're [experiencing] a story, our brain activity isn't that of an observer, but of a participant." In other words, Cron explains, "Stories instill meaning directly into our belief system the same way experience does—not by telling us what is right, but by allowing us to *feel* it ourselves... The take away is: We don't turn to story to escape reality. **We turn to story to navigate reality.**"

People who aim to take away our freedoms will always want power over our stories. We cannot let them have it.

You can encourage classroom community by having students tell stories to one another. Most of them won't realize a community is forming until it already has.

In the same way, the best way I know for writers to support rural students is to keep telling rural stories. Nuanced, complex stories with characters who allow readers to experience different ideas and ways of being. And yes, these stories may be banned in some places, but I will keep writing them. And they will continue to exist. Sometimes, just knowing that stories like theirs are out there is enough to keep a kid going.

We can show our students and readers that wielding the power of our own stories is the true definition of American freedom. We can ask thoughtful and provoking questions. We can challenge hateful beliefs in a non-threatening way, because hate almost always stems from fear. We can cut off fear's air hose in our classrooms. And we can learn ways to do that when we find community with others, sharing our own stories, triumphs, and frustrations, with fellow educators and authors.

I see you, writers and educators, transforming your own fears into strength to help young people rise above the enormous stereotypes and challenges that so many of them face.

You can forge a community that will quite literally change the world. Because all of you are teaching students who have the potential to make a positive impact on our messy and fear-filled society. Rural students might currently believe that kids like them—from the backwoods and dirt roads of our country—could never achieve the dreams they imagine. Students from any marginalized group might believe this.

But with community, they *can* achieve those dreams, even in the face of fear.

Our role, as writers and educators, is to help them believe it.

NORA SHALAWAY CARPENTER is an award-winning author, anthologist, and writing educator. Her novel The Edge of Anything was named a Best Book of the Year by Kirkus Reviews and Bank Street, and was North Carolina Humanities' selection for the Library of Congress's Discover Great Places Through Reading list. Her novel Fault Lines won the Green Earth Book Award for YA Fiction and was named to the prestigious Texas Library Association TAYSHAS State Reading List. NPR named her anthology Rural Voices: 15 Authors Challenge Assumptions About Small-Time America, to its Best of the Year list. Other accolades include the Junior Library Guild Gold Standard Selection, the Whippoorwill Award for authentic rural fiction, and the Nautilus Award championing "better books for a better world." She holds an MFA from Vermont College of Fine Arts and serves as faculty for the Highlights Foundation's Whole Novel Workshop. A neurodivergent author with an invisible disability, she champions busting stereotypes of all kinds. Visit her at noracarpenterwrites.com.

Imposter Syndrome and the Value of the Day Job

CINDA WILLIAMS CHIMA

READER QUESTION: Did you ever feel like an imposter when you first started writing? If so, how did you get past that? Thanks for any advice you're willing to give!

I started writing in third grade and published my first novel at 56. So, from a commercial standpoint, I've had plenty of time to feel imposter-ish. Perhaps I'm not the example most writers want to follow.

One way to avoid feeling like a poser is to stop begging the world for validation. Therein lies the value of the day job. A day job is not a surrender or a waste of time. A day job may be the thing that allows you to keep writing. It may be something closely tied to your heart's work—teaching, librarianship, technical writing; or it can be something totally unrelated that doesn't use up your "juice" for writing. High paying and flexible would be great, but I didn't find those kinds of jobs.

I still did work that fueled me. I worked my way through college as an advertising salesperson and copy editor. I've been a dietitian, researcher, department head, college professor, wife, and parent of two sons. Note: raising children well is a job. Anyone who says it isn't hasn't done it.

To me, a day job is more than a means of keeping food on the table and a roof over your head. It is not a way to "kill time" while you wait for success. That's not fair to those around you who deserve your full attention and effort.

One great advantage of a day job is that it provides a place to be successful when everyone is saying no to you as a writer. While publishers were turning down my short stories and agents were saying no to me as a client, I published research that helped others in my field, I established a diabetes education program, I took first-generation college students like me from self-doubt to success and graduation.

A day job is also a place to gather material for story. All writers mine their own experiences for scene, for character, for drama and plot. It is experience that gives a writer something unique to say, and experience that gives us commonality with our readers and credibility as a fellow human.

One benefit of having a day job is that you don't fall into the trap of judging your writing by its ability to support you financially. A writing teacher once told me that when your work is rejected, that rejection doesn't turn it into garbage. It has no impact on the quality of the work at all. It reflects a mismatch between writer and reader. Hold onto that, while using any feedback provided to make your work better.

Be grateful to loved ones who value what you do, but beware of the pressure of their expectations. Living with someone who is waiting for you to become a spectacular success as a writer would be, to my mind, a special kind of hell. At a writing workshop once, I spoke to a parent who had attended on behalf of her child, who had somewhere else to be (!). When Mom quizzed me for career advice for her daughter, I shared my recommendation that young writers consider how they will make a living until they can make a living as a writer. She said, "Oh, her father and I would be happy to support her until she achieves success." That gave me the shudders.

When I was a child, my mother was a great supporter of my reading and writing. The work, not its potential for fame and fortune. She passed away before my first work was published, but that didn't make her encouragement any less valuable. When I began earning real money as a writer, my husband was thrilled but also somewhat ambushed.

The downside of all of this "experience" is exhaustion, of course. Before I became a full time writer, I was getting up at 4 a.m. in order to fit writing into my other commitments to family and work. I often fell asleep on the keyboard. I all but gave up watching television and doing needlework. But I never stopped writing—poetry, personal essays, scientific papers, newspaper and magazine articles and novels. I published more and more.

I found an agent who would have me, and my first novel went to auction. My third book hit the *New York Times* list and I was offered a three-book contract. That's when I quit my day job.

I was fortunate to be married to someone with insurance, and to have enough paid work behind me to qualify for a pension one day. This year I published my fifteenth novel. Many have had a straighter path to publication than me, but I still count myself lucky to be able to do this for a living. I like to think that the meandering inefficiencies of my life pay off on the page.

I've been blessed to find an audience, but I would still be a writer even if I had not. Writing serves the writer as well as the reader. If helps us remember who we were in a different season, before today crowds out yesterday.

If there's an imposter in this business, it's the person who *is not writing*, but tells you about the great books that they'll write someday, books and stories that are much better than anything else in the market now. Stories they'll write when the market changes to value their kind of work. They'll write when their schedule clears, sometime in the future.

A writer is someone who writes, and by that measure I was never an imposter. If you are writing, neither are you.

CINDA WILLIAMS CHIMA *is the New York Times and USA Today best-selling author of the* Seven Realms, Heir Chronicles, *and* Shattered Realms *YA fantasy series. Her newest duology,* The Runestone Saga, *(HarperTeen) marries Norse mythology and magic with Viking adventure, swordplay, romance and cut-throat politics. Chima's books have received starred reviews in Kirkus and Publisher's Weekly, among others, and have been named Booksense and Indie Next picks, an International Reading Association Young Adult Choice, to the School Library Journal Best Books list, a New York Public Library Book for the Teen Age, and to the Kirkus Best YA lists. These days Cinda wanders the mountains of western North Carolina. Visit cindachima.com*

Hold onto Your (Writer) Friends in Dark Times

ROB COSTELLO

In case you hadn't heard, we recently held an election.

Sigh.

If you're anything like me, in the days and weeks since November 5, 2024, you've been struggling to breathe, let alone write. Seemingly overnight the world grew exponentially darker. I went from holding fast to the hope that we might finally walk away from the past nine years of chaos, hatred, cruelty, and lies—to watching helplessly as a slim majority of my fellow countrymen chose (with eyes wide open) to leap straight back into that same stupid abyss, dragging the rest of us down with them. It's hard to see the bottom right now. Who knows how far we'll fall or just how bleak things are about to get. I'm a horror writer, so my imagination can easily take me to some pretty nasty places.

But this is an essay about writing, not politics (though it should be said that all writing is inherently political). So, that's what I'm going to talk about: the necessity of holding on tight to your writer friends, now, as we walk through the shadow of darkness together.

Here's the thing about writing: Contrary to popular belief, it's not a solitary endeavor. Even under normal circumstances, it takes a village to write a book, and a small city to build a sustainable writing career. Your writer friends are your most enthusiastic cheerleaders when times are good, and they will stand beside you holding your hand when they're not. Though your family and loved ones may be supportive, they don't always understand what it's like to be a writer wrestling with that weird combination of crippling insecurity, exhaustive tenacity, worst-case-scenario catastrophizing, and delusional magical thinking that constitute the borderline-disordered psyches of most of us. They also have no idea how to parse and dissect the rich variety of coded micro-aggressions, embarrassing pettiness, and outright hostility we regularly experience when interacting with the wider publishing ecosystem.

Your writer friends show you how much they love you by saying the nastiest things about your critics and antagonizers. When you experience those fallow periods in your work when nothing seems to go right and you're ready to throw in the towel, it's your writer friends who will lift you up and remind you what you love most about writing. And when you achieve even your humblest of goals—the kind of thing that gets a bemused shrug from most people—your writer friends are there rejoicing in sincere satisfaction right alongside you.

Sometimes they offer more than just moral support.

For example, I probably wouldn't even be writing anymore if it weren't for Nicole Valentine, who, all the way back in 2014, asked me to join her as a teaching assistant in the Whole Novel Workshop at the Highlights Foundation. It was a particularly moribund period in my career. I wasn't writing, I certainly wasn't publishing, and yet I was watching from the sidelines as many of my friends and classmates from my MFA program were signing with agents and selling books. Becoming a part of the Whole Novel Workshop that year—and remaining a part of it ever since—offered me the community and support I needed to keep writing, just when I needed them the most.

Years later, I probably never would have tried my hand at editing my first anthology if it weren't for Nora Shalaway Carpenter, who inspired me with her work editing *Rural Voices: 15 Authors Challenge Assumptions About Small-Town America*. But it was more than just an example that Nora provided. She also gave me loads of practical advice on how to write a proposal that would appeal to publishers, how to choose contributors, how to collaborate with an acquiring editor, and how to organize a production schedule. She even showed me how to prepare for a launch and promote an anthology. It's no exaggeration to say that without Nora, *We Mostly Come Out At Night: 15 Queer Tales of Monsters, Angels & Other Creature* would not exist.

These are just two examples of the kinds of gifts my writer friends have given to me over the years. In return,

I've tried to share similar gifts with them and with many others. That's what we writers should always do for each other. Publishing is NOT a zero-sum game, although it can feel like it sometimes. Your success does not take away from mine—nor mine, yours. We need to stick together and look out for each other, because trust me, nobody else in publishing is looking out for us.

Moreover, the very best way I've found to sustain the joy and love of writing over the long haul is to share it with other people.

That was the not-so-secret agenda for the R(ev)ise and Shine! Residency I cohosted with my friends and partners Lesa Cline-Ransome, Jo Knowles, and Jennifer Richard Jacobson over Labor Day weekend in 2024. While we may have pitched it as a fun and informative retreat aimed at helping writers improve their craft, what it was *really* all about was creating a safe space for a cohort of writers to come together in community. A community that we hoped would be there for our students long after the residency was over, when they needed the help, support, and encouragement of fellow writers, as well as a team of cheerleaders to celebrate the victories, large and small, that come with the writing life. Our main goal was for our students to leave not merely with a plan for their revision, but with a whole new group of friends to sustain them on their writing journey—and in that I believe we succeeded.

The point here is that, ultimately, no matter how much success you enjoy in your writing career, you will find nothing more precious and rewarding than the other writers you meet along the way. And if these were ordinary times, that would be reason enough to cherish your writer friends. But as we all know, these are *not* ordinary times.

On Election Day 2024, lies and cynicism won. While I'll leave it to political scientists and historians to dissect the numerous reasons for this, what seems inarguable to me is that in the wake of a deadly pandemic, rampant inflation, environmental collapse, a global immigration crisis, and seemingly intractable economic and political stagnation, the mood of the country (and, indeed, much of the world) has turned bitter, cruel, and deeply mistrustful of experts and institutions. Much like Yeats's rough beast, America now finds itself slouching toward Bethlehem as we enter a self-destructive age of incivility and nihilism.

For writers (especially children's writers steeped in ideals of hope, kindness, and acceptance), this represents a profoundly frightening and dispiriting turn of events. Even before the election, we found ourselves assailed on all sides. From shrinking audiences and advances, to corporate consolidation and the mounting threat of A.I., in recent years the publishing landscape has looked more and more like a battlefield. Add to that the rising politicization of books, libraries, and basic Constitutional rights like freedom of speech and expression, and it sometimes feels as if we writers are little more than cannon fodder defending hopeless ground in a full-scale onslaught against truth and decency. I won't lie: I fear for us. I fear for our livelihoods, our freedoms, our books, our lives. I fear for our families and our friends. Which is precisely why, in a country that has seemingly given up on everything we value and hold dear, we need desperately to cling to each other if we have any hope at all of not giving up, too.

Because that would be the easiest thing to do right now, wouldn't it? The safest thing. The sensible course of action. Why not walk away from the truth when telling it might get us banned or even arrested? Why not turn our backs on writing when there's no profit in it anymore? Why not keep our heads down and our mouths shut as the world falls apart around us? These are the kinds of terrible questions we may well face in the years ahead, as we witness atrocities and injustices and feel the full weight of political oppression bearing down upon our necks.

To be clear, I'm not here to judge anyone who ultimately takes the path of least resistance. We're storytellers, after all, not martyrs. We don't owe the world our blood. But for those of us who choose to take up the fight, I believe the writing communities we form will prove vital and sustaining in ways we can barely even comprehend right now—financially, legally, emotionally, and psychologically.

For my own part, I've felt empowered by supporting groups like Authors Against Book Bans and We Need Diverse Books. I've been uplifted by conversations with my close writer friends—so much so that we've established monthly Zoom meetings to check in on each other and make sure we're doing okay. And through the platform of R(ev)ise and Shine!, I've taken action with my partners to build a thriving writing community that we hope will continue to offer solace and motivation to writers all across the country.

In a world that has eagerly embraced madness, I believe it is only our fellow writers who can keep us grounded and in touch with that part of ourselves that makes us who we are. I remain hopeful that this era of political nihilism will soon pass; that cynicism, lies, and self-dealing will quickly prove poor substitutes for responsible governance; that voters will come to their senses before it's too late. But no matter what happens in the years ahead, I urge my fellow writers to hold on tight to your writer friends and communities, because we're going to need each other like we've never needed each other before.

In community,
Rob Costello, December 7, 2024

ROB COSTELLO (he/him) *writes contemporary and dark fiction with a queer bent for and about young people. He's the contributing editor of* We Mostly Come Out at Night: 15 Queer Tales of Monsters, Angels & Other Creatures *(Running Press Teens), named a 2024 CYBILS Award Finalist, as well as a Notable/Best Book of 2024 by the New York Public Library, Ginger Nuts of Horror, PseudoPod, and Reactor Magazine. He's also author of the short story collection* The Dancing Bears: Queer Fables for the End Times *(Lethe Press), named a finalist for The Whirling Prize. His debut novel,* An Ugly World for Beautiful Boys, *is forthcoming from Lethe Press. His stories have been nominated for the Pushcart Prize and have appeared in* The Dark, The NoSleep Podcast, The Magazine of Fantasy & Science Fiction, PseudoPod, Hunger Mountain, Stone Canoe, Narrative, *and* Rural Voices: 15 Authors Challenge

Assumptions About Small-Town America (Candlewick). An alumnus of the Millay Colony of the Arts, he holds an MFA in Writing from the Vermont College of Fine Arts and has served on the faculty of the Highlights Foundation since 2014. He is co-founder (with Lesa Cline-Ransome, Jo Knowles, and Jennifer Richard Jacobson) of the R(ev)ise and Shine! writing community, and he lives in upstate NY with his husband and their four-legged overlords. Learn more at: www.cloudbusterpress.com & www.revise-and-shine.com.

Missed Connections, Misunderstandings, and Misbeliefs: Two Out of Three Ain't Bad, But They Could Be Better

DAVID MACINNIS GILL

Conflict is the engine that keeps a story running, throwing characters into action, testing their limits, and making readers hang on every twist and turn. Of the many ways to stir up trouble in a narrative, three stand out: missed connections, misunderstandings, and misbeliefs. Each has its merits, but let's be honest—some work better than others. Missed connections may feel like a trick to stretch the plot, and misunderstandings can be maddeningly simple to resolve, but misbeliefs, oh boy, they dig deep into a character's soul, and leave a lasting impression on the reader, offering deeper character insight and emotional payoff.

Part 1: Missed Connections – A Frustrating Delaying Tactic

Missed connections are a classic storytelling tool, where characters barely fail to meet or exchange critical information due to bad timing, coincidence, or some external obstacle. On the surface, this kind of conflict might seem like an easy way to create suspense or prolong a narrative. After all, who doesn't feel frustrated when two characters we're rooting for come *so close* to finding each other, only to miss out by a hair? But here's the catch: while missed connections can temporarily heighten tension, they often leave readers or viewers feeling cheated. Why? Because the outcome usually doesn't depend on the characters' actions, choices, or growth—it depends on sheer luck. And when conflict resolves itself based on luck rather than character agency, the story risks losing its emotional impact. The problem with missed connections is that they often lack substance. Sure, they can create stakes—will the characters finally meet?—but the stakes are shallow because they don't stem from the characters themselves. Instead, they're imposed by the plot, which can make the whole situation feel artificial.

Every author probably has that one moment when they realize the conflict of a film or novel is hanging by a thread of convenience rather than substance. For me, it happened while watching the Shirley Temple film *Heidi* (1937). The plot revolves around Heidi being separated from her beloved grandfather, setting up a series of painfully contrived near-misses to keep them apart.

At one point, Heidi is whisked away to Frankfurt, and despite her best efforts to return, fate seems determined to thwart her. While this prolonged separation raises the stakes—will they ever reunite?—it relies entirely on coincidence and bad timing. As a kid, I remember feeling more annoyed than invested. After the third just-missed, I gave up and changed the channel. Sure, the memory stuck with me, but not in the way the filmmakers had intended.

Missed connections also play a role in Delia Owens' *Where the Crawdads Sing* (2018), though the stakes feel more personal. The novel follows Kya, a girl abandoned to survive alone in the North Carolina marshes, whose life is shaped by her isolation. A significant part of that loneliness comes from the missed opportunities between Kya and Tate, her first love. Tate leaves for college and fails to return as promised, leaving Kya to feel abandoned once again. While this separation adds to her emotional walls and deepens her character, it's hard to ignore that Tate's failure to communicate feels like an easy, avoidable way to create conflict. He could've written a letter or sent word, but the story demands that he doesn't, leaning on the missed connection as a plot device instead of letting their choices drive the drama.

Similarly, *The Rosie Project* (2013) by Graeme Simsion uses missed connections as a recurring theme. Don Tillman, a socially awkward professor, sets out to find a perfect partner through his highly logical "Wife Project." Along the way, he meets Rosie, who doesn't fit his criteria but challenges his worldview in ways he doesn't expect. While their relationship grows over time, the story leans on Don's rigid thinking and failure to act to create tension. There are moments when Don narrowly avoids realizing his feelings for Rosie, often because he's too stuck in his own head. These delays are charming at first, but they start to feel like artificial barriers rather than genuine obstacles. You root for Don and Rosie, but you can't help wishing the plot trusted their emotional connection enough to drive the story without the missed opportunities.

Erin Morgenstern's *The Night Circus* (2011) takes the idea of missed connections to a more ethereal level. The novel follows Celia and Marco, two magical rivals caught in a high-stakes competition, whose love story is marked by their inability to truly connect. Instead of meeting directly, they often communicate through intermediaries or experience each other's presence indirectly through their enchanted circus. While this separation adds to the novel's dreamlike atmosphere, it can also frustrate readers. The tension between them is less about the choices they make and more about the external circumstances keeping them apart. As a result, their romance feels delayed rather than driven by the stakes of their magical duel, leaving the reader longing for more agency in their relationship.

And then there's *Home Alone* (1990), a classic holiday film where missed connections become the foundation for comedy. Kevin McCallister is accidentally left behind when his family rushes to the airport for a Christmas trip to Paris. While Kevin faces his own adventures defending the house from burglars, his mother spends the film in a series of chaotic attempts to reunite with him. The humor and charm of the movie make it easy to forgive the implausibility of a family forgetting their youngest child, but let's be honest—if this were a drama, it would feel ridiculous. The conflict is entirely accidental, not driven by meaningful choices, and while it works for a lighthearted farce, it would be hard to take seriously in a story with deeper emotional stakes.

Speaking of romantic comedy, *Serendipity* (2001) takes the concept of missed connections to its extreme. Jonathan and Sara have a magical first meeting but decide to let fate determine whether they're meant to be together. Instead of exchanging contact information, they leave their future in the hands of the universe. The film's tension comes from years of near-misses as they cross paths but never quite meet again. While the premise is whimsical, it's also frustrating because the conflict relies entirely on coincidence. There's no growth or choice involved—only arbitrary delays. The result is a story that feels charming but shallow, as though the characters are waiting for the plot to catch up to them rather than shaping their destinies. Missed connections might work in small doses, but relying on them too heavily can backfire. When conflict isn't rooted in the characters' decisions, it risks alienating the audience. Stories are at their best when characters participate in their struggles.

Part 2: Misunderstandings – Conflict Falling Flat

Misunderstandings are a classic go-to for creating conflict, but let's be honest—they can be hit or miss. Sure, they're great for stirring up tension when characters misinterpret each other's motives or actions, but when the resolution boils down to something as simple as, "Why didn't they just talk to each other?" it can leave readers or viewers feeling cheated. For a misunderstanding to work, it needs to dig deeper, revealing something meaningful about the characters or their relationships. Otherwise, it risks coming off as a cheap way to stretch the story.

In the film *Crazy, Stupid, Love* (2011), the whole tangled mess of assumptions between Cal, his son Robbie, and everyone else is hilarious, but let's face it: the central misunderstanding is pretty flimsy. Robbie thinks his dad is getting back together with his mom, but Cal is dating someone new. Cue the chaos. It's funny, sure, but also frustrating because one honest conversation could've cleared up the whole thing way before the big, climactic showdown. Instead of feeling like an organic conflict, it's more like a sitcom setup.

Now look at the movie *The Notebook* (2004). This one leans on a more dramatic misunderstanding, but it's no less exasperating. Allie's parents intercept Noah's letters, making her think he's abandoned her. That deception drives years of heartbreak and separation, but it's hard not to feel like the conflict is a little too manufactured. It's not really about Noah and Allie's choices or flaws—it's about meddling parents. The drama is there, but it doesn't feel earned in the same way as a conflict that comes from the characters themselves.

Sometimes, misunderstandings are played for laughs, like in the animated movie *Shrek* (2001). When Shrek overhears Fiona calling herself a "hideous beast," he assumes she's talking about him. Instead of clearing things up, he retreats, derailing their budding romance. It's a classic case of a problem that could've been solved with a single, straightforward conversation. The misunderstanding fits the movie's lighthearted tone, but even in a comedy, you can't help but think, "Seriously, Shrek? Just ask her what she meant."

On the other hand, misunderstandings can be used to explore a character's deeper struggles, as Gail Honeyman does in her novel *Eleanor Oliphant Is Completely Fine* (2017). Eleanor isn't just misinterpreting people for the sake of the plot—her misunderstandings stem from her profound loneliness and inexperience with social norms. When she mistakes her coworker Raymond's kindness for politeness or convinces herself that a musician she barely knows is her soulmate, it's not just frustrating—it's heartbreaking. Her missteps reveal so much about her inner world that you can forgive the fact that clearer communication might have resolved some of the tension sooner.

In Liane Moriarty's novel *Big Little Lies* (2014), misunderstandings create layers of tension across an entire community. Jane is ostracized because of assumptions about her past, while Celeste hides the truth about her abusive marriage, leading others to misinterpret her actions. These misunderstandings build suspense, but they also rely heavily on characters withholding information, sometimes unnecessarily. When people could just say what's really going on but don't, it risks feeling contrived.

Finally, in Shari Lapena's novel *The Couple Next Door* (2016), misunderstandings are front and center in a kidnapping mystery. Anne and Marco, a couple dealing with marital issues, constantly misread each other's actions and emotions. Anne suspects Marco of hiding something, while Marco struggles to figure out what's going on with Anne. The tension is palpable, but at times, the misunderstandings feel forced—like they're there to create drama rather than having it grow naturally from the characters' flaws or fears.

When misunderstandings work, they add depth by showing us what's really going on beneath the surface. But when they're overused or too easily resolved, they can feel like lazy storytelling, leaving the audience wishing the characters would just, y'know, talk.

Part 3: Misbeliefs – The Power of Flawed Perception

Misbeliefs are where storytelling gets interesting. Unlike misunderstandings or missed connections, they come straight from a character's internal world—what they believe about themselves, others, or how life works. And here's the thing: they're wrong. Watching characters act on those false beliefs, with all the unintended consequences that follow, is one of the most powerful ways to create tension and emotional depth in a story. When their misbelief finally unravels, it's like the whole world shifts, not just for the character but for the audience, too.

Take *The Sixth Sense* (1999). Dr. Malcolm Crowe spends the whole movie trying to redeem himself by helping a boy who claims he can see dead people, all while carrying around the misbelief that he's alive. When the truth hits—that Malcolm is dead—it's devastating.

Every choice he's made, every interaction, suddenly takes on a whole new meaning. It reframes everything about the story and makes you feel for Malcolm in a way you didn't expect.

Then there's *Big Fish* (2003), which tackles misbelief in a completely different way. Will Bloom grows up thinking his dad, Edward, is full of it—a compulsive liar who's made a career out of telling tall tales. Will's misbelief drives their estrangement and his skepticism about Edward's stories. But as Will digs deeper into his father's life, he starts to see the truth behind the fantastical stories, and it changes everything. By the end, Will doesn't just reconcile with his dad. He embraces the magic Edward saw in the world. It's heartwarming and bittersweet, all because the story leans into Will's flawed perspective.

Pixar's *Coco* (2017) gives us another take on misbelief, this time through Miguel, a kid who idolizes the famous musician Ernesto de la Cruz. Miguel is convinced Ernesto is his great-great-grandfather and his ticket to understanding his own passion for music. But when Miguel learns the truth—that Ernesto is a murderer who betrayed Miguel's ancestor, Héctor—it's a gut punch. Suddenly, Miguel has to rethink everything he values, and the stakes of the story shift from hero worship to reclaiming his family's true legacy. It's a perfect example of how misbelief can drive a plot while also digging into themes of identity and belonging.

On a more intimate scale, Ian McEwan's *Atonement* builds its tragedy on a single, devastating misbelief. Briony Tallis, a young girl, sees something she doesn't fully understand between her sister Cecilia and Robbie Turner. She jumps to the wrong conclusion, accusing Robbie of a crime he didn't commit, and the fallout destroys lives. Briony's misbelief isn't malicious—it's born from her naivety and limited understanding of adult relationships. As she grows older and realizes the damage she's done, her guilt becomes the heart of the story, making her quest for redemption both moving and impossible.

Sometimes, misbeliefs make us question everything, like in Yann Martel's *Life of Pi* (2001). Pi Patel spends months stranded on a lifeboat, convinced he's sharing it with a tiger named Richard Parker. This belief shapes his survival strategies and gives him a strange kind of companionship. But by the end, we're left wondering: was the tiger even real? If not, what does that say about Pi's story—and about the human need to create meaning in the face of suffering? It's a misbelief that doesn't just define the character. It pulls the audience into a bigger, existential conversation.

Even villains aren't immune to misbelief, as *Gone Girl* (2012) brilliantly shows. Amy Dunne is convinced that her husband, Nick, has wronged her in some fundamental way, and this belief fuels her diabolical revenge plot. Amy's narcissism and entitlement distort her reality, turning her into one of the most chilling and unforgettable antagonists in modern fiction. Her misbelief isn't random—it's twisted but consistent with her worldview, which makes her actions terrifyingly believable.

Misbeliefs don't just shape characters. They can define entire narratives, sometimes flipping our expectations of who the protagonist really is. In *Avengers: Infinity War* (2018), Thanos operates under one of the most colossal misbeliefs in modern storytelling. He's convinced that the universe's suffering is due to overpopulation and that the only solution is to erase half of all life. To him, this isn't an act of villainy—it's mercy. Thanos genuinely believes he's the hero of the story, sacrificing everything, even his beloved daughter Gamora, to bring what he sees as balance to the universe.

Thanos' story is compelling because it centers on his misbelief. While the Avengers are trying to stop him, *Infinity War* frames Thanos as the one driving the action, the character with the clearest goal and the greatest sacrifices. An insightful viewer might even argue that Thanos is the film's protagonist—he's the one whose beliefs and decisions shape the narrative. And yet, his misbelief is devastatingly flawed. He fails to see that his solution doesn't address the root causes of suffering and that his self-appointed role as the universe's savior is a horrifying abuse of power. When he succeeds in his mission, the emotional weight of his misbelief is staggering. The audience isn't just horrified by the snap—it's the realization that Thanos truly believes he's done the right thing that makes the ending so haunting.

Misbeliefs are personal. They don't rely on coincidences or poor communication. They come straight from the way a character sees the world, even when that perspective is flawed. Watching those beliefs unravel—whether through tragedy, redemption, or shocking revelation—creates moments that stay with us long after the story ends. Misbeliefs remind us that the most profound conflicts aren't about what happens to a character but what's happening inside them. And that's where the magic is.

Conflict is the backbone of storytelling, but not all conflicts are created equal. Missed connections might serve a purpose now and then, but they often feel contrived, dragging the story out with delays that don't let the characters take charge. Misunderstandings can generate drama, sure, but they run the risk of frustrating readers when the resolution feels too simple—like something that could've been solved with one honest conversation. Misbeliefs, on the other hand, are where the magic happens. They dig deep into a character's psyche, showing us how flawed perceptions shape their decisions. When misbeliefs unravel, they reveal emotional truths and thematic depth that resonate long after the final page or scene. By centering stories on the flawed yet sincere beliefs of their characters, authors can craft narratives that feel personal, compelling, and unforgettable—the kind of stories that stick with us, challenging us to see the world differently.

DAVID MACINNIS GILL is the creator of The Sticky Note Plot method and the award-winning author of Three Sisters, Zombie Train, Uncanny, Black Hole Sun, Invisible Sun, Shadow on the Sun, Rising Sun, and Soul Enchilada. His books have been named ALA Best Book for Young Adults, Kirkus Best Books, Bank Street College Best Books of the Year, and an NYPL Stuff for the Teen Age. His short stories, essays, and poetry have appeared in many journals, magazines, and anthologies. He lives near Asheville, NC. Visit him at davidmacinnisgill.com & stickynoteplot.com

Life in Small Doses

HALLI GOMEZ

You know that insufferable person who loved book reports and essays in high school? That's me. The intelligence analyst who made up reports just so they could write them? Also me. And yes, I am aware I just admitted to being in the unpopular crowd.

Most people prefer writing in small doses. I am not most people. I love to write. After all, an assignment to write two paragraphs is an opportunity to write two paragraphs! I love the creative process in whatever form it takes. Long, short, whether it's an essay, a novel, or filming a video describing why *Psycho* is the most perfect movie. I love words, dialogue, and creating new adventures.

So, knowing what you know now about me, imagine what it would be like if I did not have the ability to write. If I was unable to physically put pen to paper or fingers to keyboard.

A little more background is necessary here. I have Tourette Syndrome. It is a neurological disorder characterized by motor and vocal tics that may change over a person's lifetime but do not completely disappear. In layman's terms, my body moves a lot: jerking motions, neck twitches, hand squeezes, and sometimes I sound like I'm humming. That's what it looks and sounds like on the outside. On the inside, there are times when it feels as if bugs are crawling around my organs and through my veins. Gross right? Yeah, I can't lie, it doesn't feel good.

Enough of that. I was talking about writing. For most of my life, the Tourette hasn't interfered with my writing. We've co-existed for years and the disruptions have been minor. For example, at times I walk slowly because I lift my leg at odd angles, have muscle pain from overuse, and I can't wear jewelry without it creating uncomfortable sensations on my skin. As I said, minor. Until now.

The tics are now located in my right hand and torso and get so bad I physically can't write or type. And I just stated a new novel! A young adult horror about a monster who crawls out from under the main character's bed and wants to be friends. I am over-the-top excited. I have twenty-five pages of notes and an outline. I'm ready to begin writing the first draft.

But I can't sit still. Anything over five minutes is too long. I can't stand still either so writing standing up is not an option.

For a while, I couldn't see past the hopelessness. I've

had tics that lasted for years. What if these tics lasted that long? I was terrified that if they didn't change, I'd never write again. Not an essay like this, not the many ideas for novels percolating in my mind, or even a note to a friend. But I couldn't give up writing. My brain and heart wouldn't let me.

One day when I was struggling to write, I decided to give my brain and body a break. I paced the house for ten minutes until I was calm enough to sit back down. I managed to get a few words on the paper then took another break. Wait. Did I just find a solution? I believe I did! Hooray!

My new routine is to write for five minutes then pace the house for ten. Write for five. Pace for ten. This has been going on for four weeks. After the first week to make my pacing more interesting—because how many times can you walk the same rooms and hallway—I started kicking a ball around (a little indoor soccer) and playing with the nunchucks and kamas I used when I was on the demo team at my taekwondo dojo.

Frustrating sure. But hey, I lost four pounds! This is me trying to find positivity in small doses.

Because let's face it, it's devastating for an author to be unable to write. Whether it's from writer's block or stress from a deadline, having a shiny new idea and not being able to bring it to life isn't what you want or need.

These tics are hanging around a while, but I refuse to let them stop me. And I refuse to stop writing. As I said, I write for five minutes at a time. Sometimes it's a few words, other times a few sentences. I send myself short texts with ideas, write a sentence on napkins or post it notes if that's all I have. Because I know that as suddenly as the tics changed for the worse, they will change to something workable, as tics do with this disorder. And when they finally do and my body allows me to sit for thirty minutes at a time, I will gather those texts and notes and begin putting paragraphs together.

There should be a lesson or words of wisdom in this essay besides stay out of classes with Halli because she's already pissed off former classmates.

Not much is constant or forever. Tourette syndrome is. Me being that annoying student who gasps with excitement when the teacher assigns essays is. And for me, writing is too.

But for now, I've learned to love life in small doses. Whether that's a brief break in the clouds on a rainy day, a few days with my kids who are now adults, or a good book that I know will eventually come to an end. Or a few precious moments spent writing.

Halli Gomez
Charlotte, North Carolina
December 22, 2024

HALLI GOMEZ writes stories for children and young adults with neurodivergent characters including her award-winning young adult novel, <u>List of Ten</u>. She works at her local independent bookstore, reads, and breaks out of escape rooms with her family. Halli lives in North Carolina with her husband, two kids, and two dogs.

Counting Beads

ROBIN GOW

I am not a patient person. My brain usually feels like one of those bingo-ball tumblers, constantly churning through worries and ideas and stray memories. Because of this, it always surprises me when, seeing my beadwork, people often say, "I would never have the patience for that."

I'm equally not a very patient writer. I write every day in short spurts and revision has always been my least favorite part of the process. When I first started writing I always thought it would get easier and easier the more books I wrote, but I have actually found it completely the opposite. With my last few projects, I've felt like I have fewer answers than ever about what it means to be a writer and how to tell stories with the layers of nuance and knotted-ness we all experience.

My partner and I took an Indigenous-led beading

class on a whim. I've always loved art but I've never been really great at it. Still, it seemed fun and also a good way to connect with the Indigenous parts of our heritage to learn a new skill. My partner is Choctaw, Muskogee, and Cherokee descendant and I am a descendant of the Umatilla as well as Cañari people.

As a testament to my impatience, I actually didn't complete any of the pin we were supposed to work on in the workshop. I have always struggled with doing tasks "in class" but I loved to watch. My partner picked it up instantly. I witnessed his hands move, passing needle through felt. Beads spun around the cabochon and when we got home, he kept working. I loved seeing what he could do and, in a bit of an out-of-character moment, I started watching videos to remind myself of what the instructor had said in the workshop and I started to pick it up too.

Beadwork came to me in a time I really needed something new in my creative life. I had just left my day job to be a writer full-time and I felt unworthy and unmarred. A terrible voice would whisper to me, "What makes you think you are so special that you can do this for a living?" I found a wonderful and freeing answer in beadwork. Working as a creative person in a capitalist world, we learn to tie so much of our worth to how much money we make and how much we can produce. Then, likewise, those very things are what determine if we can survive or not. The instructor of the beadwork class started the talk by showing slides of beadwork going back to the 1800s from her nation (Comanche). They were a testament to the ways art and stories have always been not just why we survive but how we survive. I am not special because I am an individual, I am special because what I create is a sum of all that's been created before me and what is still being created around me and in my community.

I feel grateful for how much I've learned through each piece I bead on. I tighten the rows of seed beads. I learn new ways to make edging and new stitches. Often, I make mistakes that require me to undo whole chunks of work. Beadwork shows me tangibly what it means to not let go of the thread. Often in writing projects I feel like a failure when I don't get a draft right the first time. It's absurd to think that anyone could do that but I find I am harsh to myself. Beading teaches me that patterns and patience hold beautiful designs and fresh futures. It also reminds me that all our stories are flowing into a history of story-telling. I imagine a web of beads, glimmering, each a grain of resilience.

ROBIN GOW is an autistic bisexual genderqueer poet, educator, and witch passionate about queer and disability justice. Awarded the Jerry Cain and Scott James Creative Writing Fellow, Gow earned faer MFA in Creative Writing from Adelphi University where fae also taught as a professor of English. Gow is the author of the YA novels in verse <u>A Million Quiet Revolutions</u> and <u>Ode to My First Car</u> with FSG Books for Young Readers and <u>Dear Mothman</u> with Abrams Books. His MG novel <u>Gooseberry</u> is forthcoming May 2024 from Amulet. Robin's chapbooks for adults include <u>Honeysuckle</u> (Finishing Line Press), <u>Backyard Paleontology</u> (Glass Poetry), <u>A Museum for That Which No Longer Exists</u> (forthcoming 2024 from Alternating Current Press), as well as the collections <u>Our Lady of Perpetual

Degeneracy (Tolsun Books), *Lanternfly August* (Driftwood Press), and *the moon crawls on all fours* (Weasel Press). Over the last five years, Robin has trained over 3,000 people on LGBTQIA2+ Inclusion and Equity and Neurodiversity/Disability Justice topics.

Social Thrillers

ALAN GRATZ

I get a ton of fan mail from young readers about my books, which I love. The best ones are from middle schoolers who say, "I've read every one of your books and I can't wait for more!" Or high schoolers who say, "I never finished a book until I read *Code of Honor,* and now I've read it four times."

The worst letters—usually e-mails that come in about ten o'clock at night—say things like, "I have a book report due tomorrow. Can you tell me the theme of *Projekt 1065?*" or "I have to find five quotes each about perseverance and coming of age in *Refugee,* but I can't find any. Can you please give me some examples with page numbers?" (That was an actual e-mail I got. It was the girl's assignment to show why she should get into advanced English.)

I get a lot of letters and e-mails from teachers and

librarians as well—and the best part is, they almost never ask me what the themes of my books are. Instead they tell me things like, "I started reading your book out loud to my class and they beg for more every time I have to stop," or "A student came to me and told me I had to read your book, and told all his friends they had to read it too."

When I started to get letters like that, and the good ones from young readers, I stepped back and tried to figure out what it was I was doing right—because obviously I wanted to write more books like that. It's not like I'd started writing books for young readers with any kind of plan or agenda. I didn't, for example, set out to write books for "reluctant readers." (Or, what educator and reading advocate Donalyn Miller calls "dormant readers.") I was just writing the kind of books I wanted to read now, and would have wanted to read when I was a kid.

But when I think back on my own childhood, I realize that *I* was a dormant reader. Which is odd to say, because I was also a *good* reader. That is, my reading comprehension skills, my vocabulary, my attention span, they were all good enough that I was able to read and enjoy books like *The Hobbit* and *Hitchhiker's Guide to the Galaxy* in grade school. (Still two of my favorites.) But I didn't have my nose buried in a book all through middle school and high school. The truth is, I didn't read very many books on my own outside of class when I was a kid. I was more likely to be out in the woods building a fort, or playing video games, or having an adventure with my Star Wars action figures.

The point is that a book had to grab me by the collar of my Members Only jacket to compete with all the other things I enjoyed doing when I was young, and it was the rare book that managed to entice me. So when I started writing my own books, I wrote the kind of books I would have wanted to read when I was a kid. That meant getting to the story as quickly as I could—in the first chapter if possible. It meant stories with high stakes—life or death kind of stuff that really mattered. Short chapters with cliffhanger endings. Dynamic settings and relatable characters you care about.

My number one goal when I write a book is to write a book a young reader can't put down. That's what we all want, right? The kind of book you can't wait to get back to. The kind of book that you want to recommend from the rooftops. The kind of book that turns a dormant reader into an avid reader, and an avid reader into an evangelical reader. (Not...a religious evangelical reader. You know what I mean.)

But in trying to understand what it was that made kids so crazy about my books, I realized there was something more to it than just a fast plot and high stakes and short chapters and characters you care about.

I was struggling to put my finger on exactly what it was until I listened to a podcast interview with Jordan Peele, the writer and director of the movie *Get Out*. He referred to his film as a "social thriller," and that's when it clicked for me. It wasn't *just* that my books were thrilling reads. They had a social element to them too that appealed to kids. My books tackled bigger social issues beyond the thrills:

How do you make sense of senseless evil?

What is it like to be Middle Eastern in America post 9/11?

How does someone who was bullied become a bully themselves?

What is a refugee, and how could anyone turn them away?

What kind of horrors are we capable of when we demonize and dehumanize others?

What about the stories of all the marginalized people who fought and served at D-Day only to return home to face the same discrimination and prejudice and persecution they had faced before the war?

If every act of vengeance demands more revenge, how does the cycle of violence ever end?

What is "climate change," and why aren't we doing more about it?

How do the ghosts of past wars still haunt us?

And will you use your power, your strength, to help those who need it, *when* they need it, even if it jeopardizes your own personal safety?

Social thrillers. Books that entertain, but challenge young readers to think as well.

And more and more, Middle Grade readers are *choosing* to read books like mine that tackle social issues because the social issues have come to them. They've been going through Active Shooter drills since they were in elementary school. They have refugees and immigrants as classmates. They hear racist and intolerant rhetoric from political leaders on the news. They're marching in Black Lives Matter protests. Middle Grade readers don't have the luxury of thinking only about home and school and the neighborhood anymore. They are shaping their views of the larger world *right now*, in grade school, because the world is forcing them to.

That, I think, is why middle schoolers in particular have responded so enthusiastically to my books. Because beyond writing a story they can't put down, I'm also tackling questions they themselves have about the larger world. My books, like Jordan Peele's *Get Out*, are *social thrillers*. That's become my watchword. My little category on the shelf.

How do I do it? How do I tackle social issues in a way that young readers respond to? By taking statistics and giving them a name. A face.

This is Brandon. This is Reshmina. This is how Brandon crawled through a hole in the wall to escape a collapsing elevator, only to *come back* to save the other four people still trapped inside and make sure they were not among the 2,977 people who died in the Twin Towers that day. This is how Reshmina, a girl whose older sister had been killed in a US drone attack, hid a wounded American soldier in her home to make sure he was not among the more than 2,300 US soldiers who have been killed in Afghanistan since 2001.

To bring history to life, to bring a *crisis* to life, is to make it personal, to make it unique—and at the same time typical. That is the *power* of story. To turn statistics into people who come to life for us on the page. To turn numbers into characters we cry for, and care for, and root for.

Books build empathy. Empathy leads to compassion, and compassion brings change.

Books can change the world.

As just one example, let me end with another piece of fan mail, a real letter from a boy named Jack who wrote to me a few years ago.

Hi Alan Gratz,

My name is Jack. I am 13 years old, and live in Pittsburgh, Pennsylvania. I've only read *Prisoner B-3087* and your new book, *Refugee*, but I can't tell you how many times I've reread *Prisoner B-3087*. I never liked to read until my librarian recommended I check out *Prisoner B-3087*. I've always loved WWII. When I first got the book I thought the first couple of chapters were very intriguing! As I read on, this poor kid's life was pretty much failing all around him. It was horrible to find out about the concentration camps and learning what horrible things the Nazis did to these innocent people who are the exact same as you and me. Although it was a horrible time in history, I love how you "taught" it to so many kids. I loved *Prisoner B-3087*, and hope you write more books just like it.

Don't even get me started on *Refugee!!* This is easily my new favorite book of all time, and I've read a ton of books since *Prisoner B-3087*. Alan, you amaze me of how many different ways you are able to write books. I liked the constant flow of *Prisoner B-3087*, but I really like the cliff hangers at the end of each *Refugee* chapter. Then you don't get to find out what really happened until two chapters later!! Some people I know get angry about cliff hangers like that, but I watch *The Walking Dead*. I'm used to cliff hangers. Now I love when books have different people's points of view because I love to see and hear what their mind is picturing and thinking about. I am VERY impressed with *Refugee*!

You opened me up to so many different books from *Prisoner B-3087* on. I am asking for *Projekt 1065* for my birthday tomorrow! I really want all your books for Christmas. Thank you so much for opening me up to reading.

Thank you, Jack

"*Thank you so much for opening me up to reading.*"
That's what happens when a kid finds exactly the right book, at exactly the right time. That is how my books, and others like them, are building empathy in young people today, and preparing them to be readers—and leaders—for life.

Alan Gratz
Portland, OR
2024

ALAN GRATZ is the #1 New York Times bestselling author of a number of novels for young readers, including Prisoner B-3087, Refugee, Ban This Book, Allies, Ground Zero, Two Degrees, and Heroes. A Knoxville, Tennessee native, Alan and his family now live in Portland, Oregon. Visit him online at www.alangratz.com.

Room for Purple Horses: An Exploration in Finding Authentic Voice

LOCKIE HUNTER

I recently took a much-needed sabbatical from a fifteen year career in publishing to pursue my master's degree in creative writing. I didn't want to wake up at forty and realize that I had not written the great American novel. (As it so happens, I will wake up forty years old this January and will not have written the novel, but I will at least have a few chapters under my belt.) My memoir professor tells me to ask of myself: "What is the extraordinary reality that we live, that being conscious of it is enough to write a memoir of it?" My extraordinary reality includes a poet-in-residence—my three-year-old daughter Pascale.

Like most toddlers, Pascale is inquiring. She notices the veins decorating the leaves and the crow's feet stamping a pattern on my eyes. Her world is one of detection. Still, her language skills are not fully-formed.

I stalk Pascale with a pad and pencil, catching snatches of toddler verse. I'm tempted to submit some of her words as my own to one of my writing workshops. I'd get comments like, "original voice."

Milk goes after milk. But sometimes milk comes before milk.

This Ginsberg-esque poem was uttered one day when Pascale was helping her brother with his snack. It's perfect in its simplicity and its truth. If I can pattern my verse on such straightforward observations, I could make great movement towards a simpler style.

Mommy: What if I have four apples and you have four apples?
Pascale: If I have four apples and you have four apples then we will be happy and we will love each other.

Thank you, Walt Whitman junior.

It makes my stomach crumbly and it makes my stomach bumbly

Shades of E.E. Cummings here. The word bumbly is gorgeous in its descriptive powers. It evokes grumpy old men and bad haircuts. Pascale was being blunt. She did not wish to eat something, as it made her bumbly. This same frankness is what leads the child to publicly comment on indelicate items.

Mommy, that woman just picked her nose. You tell me not to pick my nose. Is it okay for grownups to pick their nose?

These candid openly-uttered comments are worth every moment of the accompanying humiliation. As parents, we all have accounts of our children's first mispronunciations. The words "purkle" or "pupple" instead of purple seems to be an almost universal memory. A girlfriend recently told me that her son waves at the ocean waves. She beamed with pride.

Are we making fun of our kids and their ignorance? No, but maybe we're feeling a mix of superiority and awe. I track my daughter and record her poems not because I wish to snicker at her mistakes, but because I know that one day her reality will be mediated, and, as such, she will utter the sayings that we all utter. Her words will become homogenized. "Have a nice day," she will say.

When I asked if she wanted a snack before dinner she said, "No thank you. I don't want to ruin my appletype."

My mother-in-law tells a story of my husband returning form school crying. He'd been given an assignment to paint a horse, and he painted it blue and purple. The teacher scolded him and told him that horses were brown. There was a painting of a carousel in my husband's house and the horses that traveled on it were shades of purple and blue. My husband was devastated at the reception his drawing received, and my mother-in-law stomped down to his school demanding to know:

"*Is there no room in the world for purple horses?*"

When playing in my off-limits room, my daughter almost overturned a framed painting that hadn't been secured to the wall yet. She came to tell me about it.

Pascale: It almost fell over and hurt me.
Mommy: That wouldn't have been good, huh?
Pascale: No. Because we're not made for that.
Mommy: For what?
Pascale: For breaking.

No. We are not made for breaking. Part of me delights in this poetry and part of me understands that my daughter will "learn to know better." Her grammar will improve; her word choices will deepen with understanding. Regardless of her future, I hope Pascale's *"original voice"* is one that will never be silenced. My writing has improved immensely since I met my daughter. She's taught me to look at the world at a slightly crooked angle, and to use my *own* words—grammatically exact or no—to tell the story of my world, my extraordinary reality. I intend to ensure that there is always room in my world, and in my writing, for purple horses.

LOCKIE HUNTER holds an MFA in creative writing from Emerson College in Boston. She serves as curator of the long-running Juniper Reading Series and co-producer of the poetry and prose radio program Wordplay on 103.3 FM in Asheville. Her words have appeared in publications including Brevity, The Baltimore Review, The North Carolina Literary Review, Hiram Poetry Review, McSweeney's Internet Tendency, Slipstream, Gulf Stream Literary Magazine, Arts & Opinion, New Plains

Review, Hip Mama and many others. Lockie's essays have been nominated for Best of the Net Awards and the John Burroughs Nature Essay Award. You can find more of her work at www.lockiehunter.com.

Motivation and Swim Buddies

JENNIFER RICHARD JACOBSON

For most of my writing life, ambition has been my motivation. I wanted to be published, I wanted readers, and I wanted recognition. And although it took determined effort and persistence, I was fortunate. I broke into children's publishing when agents were not required. Editors were open to unsolicited manuscripts and provided personal feedback if it was warranted. You could gauge your success according to the type of response you received: postcard (the worst; it meant you hadn't made it past the first reader), form letter with an actual signature, form letter with a penned note ("Not this, but keep at it!") and the coveted personal letter with a revision suggestion. Back then, we did not talk of "R&R's"—we knew a personal letter was permission to resubmit.

I was blessed to publish when editors had the time

and inclination to nurture manuscripts from rough drafts to polished gems. My writing education was not self-taught, but rather editor-taught. I honed my craft under the guidance of editors who believed in my ability, especially my knack for revision. This invaluable mentorship is not lost on me.

Additionally, more often than not, I wrote under contract. In other words, I pitched an idea to one of my editors and received not only a greenlight, but an advance to write the book. Both the interest and the financial support fueled my writing. And with these came a third gift: legitimacy. Yes, yes, many a best-selling writer continues to sell their work in this way (though I know far fewer of them). For a mid-list writer like me, this was everything.

The common question of how I maintained discipline as a writer was easily answered: deadlines and obligations. With editors (and later agents) eagerly awaiting my work, I wrote with purpose—to publish, to connect with readers, and to strive for recognition. However, the landscape of motivation has shifted dramatically in recent years.

Flashforward to today and most of these extrinsic motivations have disappeared. Due to a collision of circumstances—retirements, changes in editorial focus, and perhaps (though no one has told me this, I can surmise) books that didn't sell well—I no longer have an editor waiting for my next manuscript. I am no longer certain the stories I'm writing will be published or will find readers. My desire for accolades has taken a backseat.

And yes, I'm faced with the existential questions we

all face in later years: *Has my time come and gone? Is it time to make more room for younger, hipper, more diverse writers? Are there better things I could be doing with my hours?* But I think that the current state of the publishing industry, for reasons I won't go into here (who needs to reinforce all of the bad news of late?) has caused many of us, of all ages and experiences, to ask: If you knew your work wasn't going to be traditionally published, would you keep writing?

There was a time when I doubted it. However, experience has reshaped my understanding of what truly nourishes and sustains me as a writer, and not surprisingly, most of those aspects of the writing life are within my control.

I've learned that continual growth is a reward on its own. I suppose it's the same with anything: playing a guitar, wielding a tennis racket, gardening...the more you improve, the more you take joy in your craft. For the first time in my career, I am showing up to the page for the sheer pleasure of experimenting, sharpening, discovering. But is it enough? Enough to keep me going?

Some days.

Other days are harder to maintain forward propulsion. I am easily seduced and then beaten down by the tiniest hints of good news: a movie option (it's happened before), a nibble on an anthology (which turns out to be a pass), a book loved by my agent out on submission (crickets). Is there anything more disheartening than the constant waiting? (When I was truly young, younger than young, I used to say that by the time a boy told me he loved me, I no longer cared.

Sometimes waiting on industry professionals makes me feel the same way.) Nothing kills motivation like dashed hopes.

I've been working on an adult novel. (My brain likes the idea of a new path—which is why I have written everything from board books to young adult novels—but in this case, the path to publication is even more obscure.) Recently, I hit a place of stagnation. I typically stall because I've lost confidence, and this time was no exception. I'd begun to let the voices of imagined editors or reviewers creep in and rob me of my courage. I let a few days go by without writing (rare for me) and then, as it so happened, I attended a conference where I met up with a fellow children's author who is also writing an adult novel. Having agreed to trade manuscripts, I asked if she would be willing to read mine before it was finished.

The moment she gave me her enthusiastic yes, was the same moment I no longer needed her (yet). As I reviewed what I wanted her to know about the story, I was simultaneously feeling the power of the idea and what I still had to accomplish in order to make it work. I wanted to accomplish those things before she read it. I wanted the story to communicate on its own behalf. All I needed was the promise of a trusted reader.

Ack! How many times would I relearn this lesson? Writing, an act we consider to be solitary, is in fact quite social. During those long writing spells, when I am like Diana Nyad, crossing a vast sea without any land in sight, what I really need is a swim buddy.

There are many ways of finding swim buddies and

at different times in my career, and at different times during the same book project, I've needed different things. Sometimes my Zoom writing buddies are enough to keep me going. We sign on at the same time every day, say hello, then turn off our cameras and write in each other's company. There's an unspoken commitment to one another that keeps us showing up and our brains have become habituated to the routine. Recently, Jane Kurtz referred to this as a form of "body doubling" (a technique frequently used to assist those with ADHD) where we do what is expected of us in the company of others. It's great for getting the words on the page.

And of course, there are critique groups. Anyone who has ever had a steady critique group knows they can be incredibly helpful at providing deadlines and regular feedback, as long as there are agreed-upon protocols, and the group dynamics remain in balance. (Unfortunately, if certain understandings are not put into place, they easily devolve into a dysfunctional family system where insecurities worsen. But that's a topic for another time.)

But above all, I need a trusted reader. A reader who doesn't simply listen to snippets of my work, but is willing to give it a deep dive. Someone well-read, incredibly knowledgeable about the writing process and how story works, someone who recognizes that positive feedback is as needed and as valuable as analysis.

I began this essay by saying how lucky I was to come up in a time when editors were not as burdened as they are today. But truth be told, even then we writers would yearn for a time before ours…the time when editor Ursula Nordstrom nurtured some of the most influential writers in children's literature: Maurice Sendak, Ruth Krauss, Margaret Wise Brown, Syd Hoff, and E. B. White. This from Harper Collins' website says it all: "Nordstrom had a simple philosophy regarding new authors. As one colleague said, 'Anyone who called, anyone who got off the elevator, anyone who wrote in, could be seen and heard.' She always answered her own phone, and on hearing another ringing, would cry out, 'Answer that! That might be the next Mark Twain.'"

Who amongst us wouldn't have loved Ursula Nordstrom as a swim buddy?

Yes, publishing has changed, and editorial roles have changed, and it will continue to evolve in ways we can't predict. Deep down I know, more likely than not, I will continue to search for creative paths into that world.

But I also know I won't be wading in alone.

JENNIFER RICHARD JACOBSON has spent three decades writing award-winning fiction and nonfiction for children. Among her titles are picture books: THIS IS MY ROOM (NO TIGERS ALLOWED) *and* OH, CHICKADEE!; *chapter books:* Andy Shane *series and* Twig and Turtle *series; middle grade novels:* SMALL AS AN ELEPHANT, PAPER THINGS, THE DOLLAR KIDS, CRASHING IN LOVE; *and young adult novels:* THE COMPLETE HISTORY OF WHY I HATE HER *and* STAINED. *Her awards and honors include ALA Best Books For Young Adults, Publishers Weekly Best Books, NYPL Best Books for Teens, Parents Choice Gold Award, IRA Young Adult's Choice, ILA Social Justice Award, NTCE Charlotte Huck Honorable Mention, Bank Street Best Books of the Year, and Junior Library Guild Selections as well as many state awards. She serves on the faculty of the*

Highlights Foundation, is a board member of the Maine Writers and Publishers Association, and with colleagues Rob Costello, Lesa Cline-Ransome, and Jo Knowles, cofounded R(ev)ise and Shine!. Jennifer lives in mid-coast Maine with her husband.

Global Revision

ERIN ENTRADA KELLY

If you're a writer, you probably see a shadowy figure on the distant horizon known as *revision*. Some might call him a monster. He hovers there, waiting for you to reach the end—and when you do, he tells you it's time to return to page one. *Fair enough*, you say, knowing this day would come. Then you revisit your first chapter and think: Okay. Now what? You stare blankly at your first draft. Where do you begin? How do you know what to change? What are you supposed to look for? How can you start a global revision if you don't know what's wrong with the manuscript in the first place?

Before you begin, congratulate yourself on finishing a draft, take a deep breath, and consider doing one or all of the following:

- **Find beta readers if you can**. Ask other writers, if possible—people who understand that you want feedback on the story and structure, not commas and typos. It's helpful if the beta reader also writes in your genre, but it's not necessarily a requirement.

- **Take space from the manuscript**. Once you've finished your first draft, put it away for a while. *At least* two weeks. It's difficult to see your manuscript with an editorial eye if you don't have perspective, and distance is the only way to get perspective.

- **Understand that you may have to let go—of sentences, of scenes, perhaps even of characters—in service to your story.** Keep a separate file for those precious darlings. You may be able to use them later.

- **If you can, read your book in printed and bound form.** Distance provides perspective, but so does visual interface. You want to interact with your book as a reader as much as possible. If you've only seen your book on screen, it's helpful to see it in another form. You'll notice things you didn't see before—trust me. I realize not everyone is able to do this. But if you can, do. (Plus, it is deeply satisfying to hold those pages in your hand and know that you—yes, *you*—created all of it).

Once you've done all that, what's the next step? What questions should you ask of your work?

Scenes vs. Summary

What is the balance between scene and summary? Do you have pages and pages without any dialogue? Do you have ongoing passages with more than one character, but no one speaks? Is there a lot of telling and not showing?

Scenes are more difficult to write than narrative, so it's not surprising that writers often rely on summary to tell their stories. This is incredibly common in emerging manuscripts. Although summary clearly has a time and place in prose, you need to bring readers into the story if you want to truly engage them. Your job is to embody the story, not report it.

When I review manuscripts, I often make notes that say: "write in-scene." Basically, this means: Stop *reporting* and start *embodying*.

What does it mean to write in-scene? Typically, scenes include one or all of the following:

- Scenes happen in real time. Your readers watch events unfold, rather than being told by the narrator.
- Scenes happen somewhere, i.e. a setting.
- Something happens, whether internally or externally.
- Characters interact with their environments, often through dialogue.

Here's what summary looks like:

> When I get home, the house is dark as usual. Mom shuts the outside world away with curtains. She comes into the kitchen and pours herself a glass of scotch as I get myself a glass of water. She looks disheveled. She asks me about school and I tell her school was fine. We hardly communicate anymore.

Now let's see what this looks like in scene, as it appears in Mindy McGinnis's young adult novel, *The Female of the Species*.

> It's dark when I get home, even though the sun is still up.
>
> Our windows stay closed, our curtains drawn. It's easier for Mom to ignore the outside world this way: out of sight, out of mind, the only thing perpetually in her line of vision a bottle of scotch. I put myself in her way accidentally, our paths crossing in the kitchen as I get a glass of water. She looks up at the clock, confused.
>
> "You're home."
>
> "School lets out at three, Mom."
>
> Her eyes thin out as she squints at the clock, the shakily applied eyeliner she puts on only for

herself crimping together as she does.

"It's three-thirty," I say.

"Oh." She busies herself for a few minutes, trying to make it seem like she came into the kitchen for something other than to refill her glass. I wait her out patiently, sipping my water and crunching ice between my teeth.

"How was school?"

I imagine this question is asked all over the world, every day, receiving everything from flippant answers to in-depth reckonings. But it's hardly ever asked here, in this house.

I pulverize some ice with my molars while I think.

"School was fine," I say, and dump the rest of my water in the sink.

You don't have to turn every moment of summary into a scene. But stay attuned to those moments when you can elevate your summary to something more—something that propels the story forward, tells us something meaningful about the characters, and allows us to see and hear them interact with their environments.

Another way to identify areas where you can embrace *scene* is to pay attention to *telling* moments versus *showing*—those times when you tell us exactly what the character is seeing/thinking/feeling, rather than showing us. Yes, there are moments when telling makes more sense. But look for moments when you can show us something that brings us closer to the narrative and the character.

Here are quick examples.

Telling –

Penelope always got anxious at the frozen yogurt counter. She never knew what to get. It was so hard to make a decision. Finally, she made her choice and sat at our table.

Showing –

Penelope approached the counter.

"Strawberry, please," she said. When the guy moved toward the scooper, she waved her hands in the air. "No, no, wait! I changed my mind. I want blueberry." He shifted toward the blueberry. "No, no, wait!" Penelope said. "Sorry, I meant vanilla! Vanilla. Definitely vanilla. With sprinkles. Wait—no sprinkles. And make it chocolate."

Telling –

Trevor felt bad about what he'd said to Ebony, but he didn't know how to apologize. He tried to talk to her in the hall, but the words wouldn't come.

Showing –
"Ebony?" Trevor said. His voice sounded small in the hallway, but she must have heard him, because she turned around.

"Yeah?" she said.

Trevor clutched the strap of his backpack and looked away. He focused on a pencil on the floor. His heart thundered in his throat. "I, uh ..."

Ebony raised her eyebrows. Her mouth was a thin, flat line. "You, what?"

Trevor tried to say it. *I'm sorry, Ebony. I'm sorry.* But the words wouldn't come.

Overexplaining
I often tell writers to "cut superfluous words" or "tighten" certain paragraphs or scenes. But what does that mean, exactly? How do you recognize extraneous words in your own prose? If you wrote them, you probably thought they were necessary, right? Unfortunately, writers often don't trust themselves or their readers enough to self-edit.

Here's an example:

> Jane fidgeted in the interrogation seat and pulled at a loose thread in her sweater. When the officer narrowed his eyes at her from across the table, she looked away and focused on the discolored tile

in the corner, nervous of the look he was giving her. His glare filled the room. He was trying to intimidate her.

Pull it together, she thought.

She released the thread, straightened her back and sat still. Then she met his eyes with hers. She was scared, but trying not to show it.

It's not terrible. It's written in scene, so we've got lots of good showing. We've got some good descriptive verbs, like "fidgeted," "narrowed," "straightened." But then we've got deflating words and phrases. Three in particular:

- **... nervous of the look he was giving her.** After all that good showing (focusing on the discolored tile, not meeting his eyes), the writer doesn't trust the prose enough to let it stand on its own. Thanks to the solid technique in the preceding sentences, readers already know she is nervous. We don't need to be told.
- **He was trying to intimidate her.** This is obvious. His eyes are narrowing and his glare is filling the room. What else would he be trying to do?
- **She was scared, but trying not to show it.** We know. That's why she straightened her back and released the thread. That's why she met his eyes with hers.

I've read many well-written manuscripts with one deflator after another. It's like someone tells you a joke and then immediately scrambles to explain it, even though you got the punchline the first time. After a while you forget what the joke was even about. Worse, you forget that it was funny.

Playing "catch-up" instead of "catch-on"

Presumably, things have happened to our characters before page one that will affect how they behave, change, and evolve throughout the course of our narrative. We need to let readers know about those events so we can put our story in context.

Listen, I get it. You need to get your reader up to speed. You want them to know everything you know, and you want them to know it sooner rather than later. But imagine you're at a party, people-watching in a corner by yourself. You see an interesting person across the room. As soon as you make eye contact, they walk over and tell you their life story. You've barely said a word. How quickly would you be tired, bored, put-off, or exhausted?

Now imagine you've been secretly watching them. Maybe they talk to the fish in the tank when no one's looking, or swipe someone's wallet. Their sleeve rides up and you notice a strange and intriguing tattoo. You want to know more. You walk up closer. Maybe you ask a question and get an answer. More conversation follows. The relationship evolves *organically*.

That's what you want for your readers. Don't shove a bunch of information down their throats. Let them discover your character and your story for themselves. Think of it as opening a door into your world. They've already arrived, and you're inviting them in, showing them through the house, one room at a time.

Your opening chapter is not the place for narrative summary. Make your character active. Give them something to do.

Consider chapter one from *The Five Stages of Andrew Brawley*, a young adult novel by Shawn David Hutchinson.

> The boy is on fire.
>
> EMTs wheel him into Roanoke General's sterile emergency room. He screams and writhes on the gurney as though the fire that burned his skin away burns still, flaring deep within his bones.
>
> The boy looks my age, seventeen. His hair, where it isn't singed, is the color of autumn leaves. The kind of leaves I used to rake into piles with my dad and take running jumps into.
>
> I can't see the boy's eyes from where I'm hiding, but his voice is a chain. It grates as agony drags it out of his throat. The skin on his legs and part of his chest is charred black.
>
> The scene of burning lingers in my nose, and even as bile rises into the back of my throat, I can't help thinking of all the times I barbecued

with my family during the summer. Mom would squirrel away extra food in the back of the fridge because Dad always burned the chicken. It's late, and I should be gone, but I can't take my eyes off the boy. I'm a prisoner of his animal howls. There is nowhere in this hospital that I could hide to escape his screams.

So I stay. And watch. And listen.

As the story goes on, readers learn that Andrew, the POV character, lives in the hospital, though he isn't ill. We also learn that Andrew's family is dead, but we don't know how or why they died. Hutchinson could have used this first chapter to get us up to speed. Instead, he allows us to make these discoveries on our own, which is what keeps us turning pages. He also weaves in details that tell us what kind of family he had—*The kind of leaves I used to rake into piles with my dad and take running jumps into. / I can't help thinking of all the times I barbecued with my family during the summer.*—which makes it truly devastating when we learn how they died, and that he is the only survivor.

Read the first fifty pages of your manuscript. How much time do you dedicate to backstory or flashbacks?

Unnecessary Scenes

Each scene should be doing *something*. Ideally, each scene does more than one thing. At the end of each chapter or scene, ask yourself: What does this accomplish? If I remove it, what happens? Is there more I can do here?

Is this scene simply a filler? (I often read manuscripts where the writer says, "Well, I needed a classroom scene, so here's my classroom scene." But that's not enough. It needs to be there for a *reason*—presumably, to propel the plot and characters forward.) What happens in the scene or chapter that speaks to the next scene or chapter? What decisions are made? What new discoveries? What have we learned about the world, characters, or plot that we don't already know? How is it serving your narrative?

Another tip that I've learned over the years: If you were bored writing a scene, your reader will be bored reading it. If you find yourself bored during the drafting stage, ask yourself: Why am I writing this? Is there enough going on here? Typically, we're bored because there's nothing really happening. And if nothing is happening, why is it there?

Some think of revision as a monster—a separate beast in the writing process. But revision is *part* of writing, not a supplement to it. For me, revision is the greatest part. It's the stage where the story truly comes to life. Scenes are rewritten, deleted, or expanded. Characters become more textured. All the threads you created come together and you have a full, completed, polished manuscript sitting in your hands. Revision is about discovery. And what's more creative than that?

ERIN ENTRADA KELLY is a two-time Newbery Medalist, National Book Award Finalist, and New York Times-bestselling author whose work has been translated into more than a dozen languages. She is on faculty with the Hamline MFAC program.

Shared Light: A Love Letter to Letters

KELSEY LECKY

Dear friend,

Late at night, I write letters. A blank card balances atop my library book as I sit in bed, promising myself I won't stay up too late reading, knowing I'll break that promise every time. Letters remind me of the pleasures of writing by hand: savoring smooth paper;[1] the flow of a favorite fountain pen[2] or scrummy felt tip;[3] the depth and richness of ink;[4] the soft warmth of paper's perfume; the susurration of nib over paper.[5] Letters are an opportunity to think slowly, deeply, physically:

---

1   Crinkly sheer onionskin, smooth snowy pages.
2   Currently my Kaweco AL Sport with a pale, iridescent body.
3   Sharpie pen, always.
4   Colorverse "Mystic Mountain" at the moment.
5   Traveler's notebook lightweight paper or smooth Midori pages.

128

writing from and with my body. Writing letters is a way, for me, of inviting words in and sharing their light.

Much has been written on the benefits of writing by hand,[6] especially in cursive. In a way, letter writing tricks my brain into wanting to write more: by savoring the simple pleasure of moving pen across paper, I'm reminded of the joy of the process, both physical and creative. My notebook[7] follows me around the house after each letter, catching bits of dialogue, scenes, ideas, etc. as they come. Why? Because it's fun. It's fun to write: to watch words unspool in raspberry ink, to feel and hear the smoothness of paper under my hand, to imagine, to create. As a professional illustrator and stained glass maker, I find great joy in making. As a child, my mother and I played "make and do," and that's essentially what I still do now.[8] I write while working on stained glass, in the garden, in the pool locker room, while waiting for bread to rise, even perched on the edge of the bathtub in the middle of the night, steeping myself in the joy of creation. But for all these scriblets, letters give me the gift of stillness and quiet. They let me sink deeply into thoughts, explore ideas with no need for things to make sense. In fact, some of my favorite letters are ones where I essentially say, "I don't know." That was—is—a

---

6   Lambert, Jonathan, "Why writing by hand beats typing for thinking and learning." NPR, May 11, 2024. https://www.npr.org/sections/health-shots/2024/05/11/1250529661/handwriting-cursive-typing-schools-learning-brain

7   Traveler's notebook, brown leather. Contains a letter pad, lightweight notebook, watercolor sketchbook for stained glass ideas, and sketchbook for painting thumbnails. Plus a bear-butt charm.

8   Albeit with more boring paperwork and taxes.

powerful realization for my writing: sometimes it's more poignant, more connecting, to say, "I don't know." I say it in real life all the time; why is it so hard in writing? I have no answers, only questions examined from various perspectives. Answers are dull; give me good questions any day.

Somewhere along the way, I began to notice that good writing days followed the morning after letter writing. When I write letters, I rarely have direction or structure, and most importantly, I don't edit—either as I go or after. In a way, every letter that I write is a love letter: to my mother or friends, to paying attention—itself an act of love—to writing, to the simple pleasure of putting pen to paper. And no, before you ask, it doesn't work to write letters with the intention of bribing good writing days, at least not for me; my brain is far too persnickety for that. Writing letters reminds me why I write: to savor the joy of creation, to connect, and, most of all, to share light. It seems fitting then to share a snippet from a recent letter to my mother:

> *"I have been thinking a great deal lately about sharing light. I love Michelle Obama's book title, "The Light We Carry"; my response to her—as if we were corresponding—would be "the light we share." It's a thought both from my current manuscript and from Midwinter celebrations the world over: sharing light. Bringing light back. I was recently thinking about the upcoming People's March and if I was to carry a sign, what would it say? I searched for words that were positive, powerful, and connecting.*

Share your light.

You have so much light to share (and you share it so joyfully and generously); it's exciting to see what light will call to you, what light will grow inside you, what light will overflow life and body and habit to make the world around you brighter. What will you illuminate? Who?"

The light I share in a letter may be a momentary blip: a funny story, beautiful stamp, delightfully crinkly onionskin, even a packet of tea. But a little delight goes a long way.

My mother is my best and most faithful pen pal, our letters beginning when I was as an undergraduate as a way to remain connected while far apart. Letters for us are slow, deep conversations embellished with beautiful cards, quotes copied on slips of paper, tiny watercolors, and snippets of erasure poetry made with Sharpies and flourishes of gold ink. As a poor and car-less undergraduate unable to get to an art store or order supplies, I recycled her envelopes and cards into valentines and found-art collages which became a shared art form that we continue to this day.

Letters offer an assorted biscuit tin of small pleasures: cute stationery, lovely pens, bottles of ink, envelope doodles, sometimes wax seals[9] and ribbon, and stamps: those tiny shareable gardens of color and delight. Letters also give me opportunity to play. Games of making my handwriting resemble Elvish script remind me to hold

---

[9] I don't recommend sending wax seals through the post, unless marked as "Please hand stamp."

my pen loosely, to let words flow.[10] Design challenges of arranging text on the envelope so that curves balance one another help me experiment with composition: the sweeps of script inviting the eye to roam negative space and see possibility. Envelope doodles provide an ideal warm-up, especially on intimidating painting days. I may not feel confident enough to tackle a complex 16x20 oil painting that will eventually become a book cover, but a 5x7 envelope? That I can manage. I can coax myself with delicious pigments and different mediums,[11] letting my hand and eye loosen painting tiny bees, wildflowers, and stars. Doodles do not have to be beautiful, client-pleasing, or perfect, only fun. There is great freedom in this for me, a life-long recovering perfectionist.

Each letter is a pause, a rest. A chance for my hand to unfurl words in no particular direction. A letter provides space in which to share quiet companionship with someone. Sometimes I think of them as bits of light sent out into the world. Not that my letters are luminous or inspiring, mind you, but they are a reaching out, a spark of connection. A letter may be a small way to share light. Most of my letters may be boring jumbles of thoughts while swimming, watching clouds while driving, dog stories, but they are a form of connection. Connection invites collaboration, creativity. A letter may be an excuse to write with a new pen, a pretty card, a colorful stamp, but it is a shift—however brief—from screen to page,

---

10   Though sometimes my handwriting gets so spidery that I have to use a 0.38mm pen to print the translation of a word overtop, like furigana over kanji.
11   Watercolors, colored pencils, jars of iridescent ink, bits of collage, markers, whatever clutter is on my desk, really.

from consuming to creating, from me to you.

In contrast to the rest of my writing, I never plan letters, know rarely where, if anywhere, they're going. There's a freedom, a looseness, then that comes from spontaneous creation. Letters are an exploration, an adventure. Or a boring mull over the season, what's died in the garden this week, the disappointing book I just finished reading. Those happen too. More often than not, in fact. And that's okay. I don't edit my letters, don't draft them, don't type. Thus, letters become spaces where I am free to play, to explore, to get lost and forget the point (there's rarely a point beyond telling the person that they are loved, they are not alone, and that wonders await). With stamps. Stamps, to be sure, are one of the best parts of posting letters: delight amidst mundanity.

My fountain pen's just died, but that too is an opportunity: to experiment with new bottles of ink.[12] Letters, for me, refresh perspective. What have I noticed? When have I last paid attention? What have I perhaps overlooked? What light can I share?

All of my art, whether painting, glass, or writing, has the same aim: to share light. I deeply believe that the world needs every bit of kindness we can give. I can't fix climate change, politics, hate, or any of the other myriad challenges facing us, but I can put a tiny bit of good in the world. I can doodle silly fat animals on envelopes and perhaps make a postal worker smile, or give someone a piece of happy mail amidst bills. I can reach out to a friend with a handwritten letter to remind them that they are loved, they are thought of, and they are not

---

12 Richest, deepest midnight or a soft haze of stardust? Stardust this time, I think.

alone. I can thank writing for all the joy it's brought me by celebrating and savoring the simple pleasure of the process: hand on page, ink flowing into words, words enveloping light and sending it out into the world. And for that, dear friend, I am grateful.

    Love,
    Kelsey

KELSEY LECKY looks like a ghost and smells like a forest. She is neither. Yet. A writer, illustrator, and stained glass artisan accessorizing with a wheelchair, she lives in Asheville, North Carolina. Find her at kakleckyillustration.com.

My Foot Was Bleeding

CONSTANCE LOMBARDO

Bleary eyed from another bad night's sleep, cup of tea in hand, I stared out my balcony doors at violently swaying trees and pounding rain, listened to the wind ripping through my neighborhood, and hoped the mullioned windows would not blow out.

Hurricane Helene had landed in Western North Carolina, after two days of intense rain that had already caused our many rivers to overflow. My phone pinged with a message to evacuate. I'm on the second floor of a condo on a hill, so that felt unnecessary. I stayed put.

There had been many moments, in the three years since my divorce, that accentuated my grief and despair about being alone. This was one of the worst. If only I had a partner to hold me close and tell me everything was going to be okay. I took another sip of tea.

When the rain stopped and the winds stilled, I

stood on my balcony and peered down at the lawn, soaked, and scattered with tree branches. Not as bad as I'd imagined. Little did I know floods and gale-force winds had devastated parts of my city beyond my wildest imagination.

When I walked downstairs into the streets of my usually-manicured condo complex, the first thing I noticed was a few downed trees. We did not experience anything like the forest expanses flattened against mountainsides or the mighty old trees that had succumbed and crashed through roofs in other parts of Western North Carolina, but every fallen tree feels like losing a friend, doesn't it?

I noticed my neighbors heading down our long driveway to the main road and joined them. At the bottom, we saw our little Hominy Creek had transformed into a rushing river of incredible force, gushing over the sidewalk, flooding the road, and streaming across the intersection. The water was so deep, someone's van was almost completely submerged. The corner traffic lights were out. I suddenly felt trapped. This was my first sign Helene was not like other storms I'd experienced in Asheville. My skin prickled with a mixture of awe and fear.

When our power went out, and with it the internet, my sense of dread increased dramatically. We had running water for a few more days before it stopped, not to return for three weeks. I couldn't break the habit of turning on faucets, only to be abruptly reminded there was nothing running through those pipes.

I had two hard boiled eggs. Hummus. Olives.

Cheese. Three big bottles of water and a few containers I'd filled the night before the storm. A freezer stuffed with microwaveable meals I could not use. I realized I was sadly unprepared and would soon run out of water. I surveyed my pantry, wondering if I could stand to eat canned soup without heating it. At least there were plenty of crackers and chips.

When I opened the fridge, I did so as quickly as possible, to keep my food from rotting. After several days, with the smell getting worse seemingly by the minute, I threw everything away.

Without internet, my neighbors and I gathered like people from another time. I discovered more about them in those days than I had in three years. The guy downstairs made us breakfast sausage on his camp grill, and hot food at that moment felt like a luxury. The woman above me handed out gallon jugs of water. Another neighbor shared her worries about her mentally ill son in the next town, with whom she had yet to make contact. Someone decided the condo pool would be our source for flushing water. I had to ask how to flush a toilet with a bucket of water.

The sun set around 6:30. Time to light candles and have my flashlights at the ready. As the darkness grew, so did my fears. The shadows cast by my candles danced ominously. I read by flashlight and slept often.

My car needed gas, but stories were circulating of hours in slow-moving gas lines that stretched far down the road. Rumor had it someone had been shot in one of those lines. People were angry. And desperate.

Eventually a neighbor told me about a nearby gas

station that was manageable. So I ventured out, driving on roads with no working traffic lights. I filled my gas tank, and it felt ridiculously liberating. I drove to a hot spot at a local library, opened texts for the first time since the storm, and found a surprising number from family and friends. Their loving concern touched my heart. But what were they seeing that had them so worried?

Then I clicked onto Facebook and understood. I finally saw the shocking photos revealing the magnitude of what had happened to my beloved city.

The Biltmore area, just south of downtown, with a Wendy's sign peeking above the deluge. The River Arts District, with its funky, wonderful art studios, breweries, record shop, my favorite movie theatre, damaged beyond repair or overcome with water, debris, and toxic mud.

Videos of the French Broad River raging far beyond its banks, filled with trailers, brewery tanks, and so much debris. A circle of people holding hands in someone's living room as the water rose around them. A school bus, buildings, telephone poles, upended, twisted, moved, wrong. Places I loved, simply gone.

People I knew and people I didn't know who had lost their homes. Pets. Their neighborhood bridges and roads. Or loved ones. Or everything.

My anxiety soared. I was not in imminent danger. Still, it felt apocalyptic.

As the weeks wore on, I carried buckets of flushing water and cases of drinking water up my long flight of stairs, keenly aware of my aching shoulders. Sometimes a neighbor would help, and I was grateful. But mostly it was me, alone, trying to survive like everyone else. Of course, I had it much easier than so many others. And I also felt deep grief for my city and my loss of normalcy.

My stomach hurt. My head ached. My condo was littered with water cartons from FEMA, boasting their long shelf life. A sense of doom filled my chest. Which grocery stores were open and fully stocked? Where to do laundry? How long until our power and water returned?

Without running water, I made use of the public showers in trailers that were now stationed in various parking lots. Hot water felt like a gift. A friend said they made him feel like he was in prison. That was also true. We were thankful. We were sad. We were lost at sea.

I fought against the rising panic. I saw friends when I could and visited my ex-husband who made me tea on his little makeshift grill. Most of my neighbors eventually left, escaping one by one to places that had not been ravaged, until I was the only one on my floor. Why didn't I go somewhere too? I curled up on my couch to think about it and fell asleep to the sound of my snoring old beagle.

Was there a path back to my regular routine and my writing life?

My picture book, *Itty Bitty Betty Blob*, had come out months earlier, and I had several author events planned for October. But the local bookstores were closed because of the storm. And the highway through the Blue Ridge Mountains to Johnson City Public Library in Tennessee had been rendered impassable, plus there had been hundreds of mudslides in the mountains. Yes, there was an alternate, longer route. But I'm a nervous driver to begin with and, as I mentioned…anxiety. I cancelled that visit. The librarians were understanding and held a beautiful storytime anyway, as librarians do.

What about my late October storytime scheduled at the wonderful indie bookstore, M. Judson, in Greenville, South Carolina? That route was unaffected, and it was only an hour and change away. A dear friend agreed to go with me. She drove. We agreed her title for the day was "Author Handler."

We talked nonstop the whole way there, about the hurricane, of course, and how we were dealing or not dealing, and how we were definitely not okay. She told me about the tree that had fallen near, but not hit her house, and about the dead bird that had appeared in her toilet-flushing water bucket on her birthday. We laughed. Gallows humor!

Like the release of a lifted pressure valve, it felt good to let it all out. We talked with grief-filled voices about how the raging rivers had taken so many lives, and destroyed so many homes, so much artwork, and businesses, including our favorite taco place, where you could enjoy delicious food at their picnic tables by the river. We talked about the Search-and-Rescue missions underway, the constant whirr of helicopters overhead, so many people lost. We wondered if Asheville could rebuild after what they were calling a "once in a thousand years" hurricane.

And then we pulled into a parking garage in Greenville. A lovely city with a vibrant downtown. As we made our way into the street, we both felt it, like a gut punch. The stark contrast had a *Twilight Zone* quality. We were about to enter another dimension, one where stores were open, with cheerful "Welcome" signs and invitations to sample things. Where water was readily available. Where people smiled and laughed, deciding where to lunch: crepes, pizza, or dumplings?

Clearly, we weren't in Asheville anymore.

We walked to the bookstore, housed in the historic Greenville County Courthouse, white brick, tall, and impressive. We were a little early, and I saw my chance to get a latte, an indulgence I hadn't experienced in weeks.

Inside, we were warmly welcomed by friendly booksellers whose shoulders were not hunched in worry. Whose hair looked freshly washed, faces freshly scrubbed. I used the restroom and had a hard time tearing myself away from the running, uncontaminated, miraculously hot water.

And then it was storytime, part of a series dubbed "Cookies over Books"—with oversized, Halloween-themed sugar cookies. Children arrived dressed like superheroes and princesses. I sat down on my storyteller throne, looked at all the beautiful, eager faces of children ready to get lost in a good book, and realized the challenge of this situation: get through storytime without bursting into tears.

My emotions, very front and center to begin with, had been percolating madly ever since the hurricane. In Asheville, I'd been stuck in freeze mode, overcome with fear, grief, and survivor's guilt.

But now it was time to be here, to be a good storyteller, here with these children.

These children, sitting before me with their big eyes

and neatly combed hair, had not, thankfully, lost their homes, their schools, their libraries, and even entire neighborhoods. They did not worry where clean drinking water or their next meal would come from. They did not know about the mother who lifted her child to safety, moments before being carried away by the rushing river, as she uttered her final, "I love you," to her child.

I did. I knew. I felt it in my bones. I thought of her, and all the grieving families and communities, and took a deep, calming breath. Time to focus. I opened my book.

The children seated before me on floor cushions listened, and giggled, and squirmed. Some talked while I read, like little kids do. I usually pause to look at an attentive kid and say, "I really appreciate that you're being a good listener." But this one little boy right in front of me just kept talking, insistently, repeating one line over and over.

Finally, I stopped, looked at him, and said, "Yes?"

He held out his leg for me to behold. "My foot was bleeding."

Here was the piece of information he so desperately needed me to hear. I saw no evidence of blood or even a band-aid. He was obviously fine. And yet these words, on my fraught nerves, could have pushed me over the edge and into the pool of tears waiting just behind my eyeballs. Just the suggestion of harm. It was almost too much.

But I was in Greenville, in a lovely bookstore. And this boy and all my young listeners were healthy, whole, and safe. Everything in me bubbled up and out in the form of laughter. Possibly manic laughter, but still.

I kept reading my book, about a happy little blob who is irrepressibly herself. Who learns to celebrate all that she is, with the help of friends and a supportive mom. I stood and asked everybody to move like blobs with me, all together. And we did, all of us undulating joyfully. It was glorious.

Afterwards, my friend and I went out for pizza and then drove back to Asheville. "That was great," I said. "Yes," she said. "It really was." I felt lighter. And stronger.

A few weeks later, the election results brought this experience into a sharper light. Because there are those in power who want to squash the stories. Their book banning agenda sends a clear message to children: you are not allowed to be who you truly are, your families, if they differ from what we consider "normal," do not matter, your history should be forgotten. They want to silence all voices that celebrate anything outside of their own narrow, bigoted lives.

I'm a writer who chooses to write for children. And I will continue to bring them stories about compassion, collaboration, and celebrating our differences. I will continue to strive to bring them hope, laughter, and joy. I want them to know that I see them. And I love them.

Maybe I can't stop hurricanes. Or the destructive hatred and oppression of the incoming administration. But we writers can do something powerful, magical. We can bring to life tiny blobs who shine bright in a world of monsters. Muscular bulls like Ferdinand, who choose flowers over fighting. Children who speak with pride about their two mothers' house, where love flows abundantly.

I will write for and read to children as long as I can. Come hell or high water, or even both at the same time.

December 2024
Constance Lombardo

CONSTANCE LOMBARDO is the author/illustrator of three middle grade novels about Mr. Puffball, the stunt cat. Her picture books are <u>Everybody Says Meow</u>, <u>Tiny Spoon vs. Little Fork</u>, <u>Itty Bitty Betty Blob</u>, and <u>Itty Bitty Betty Blob Makes a Splash</u>. She is also the recipient of a North Carolina Arts Council Artist Support Grant for her zine, Please Be Small, Adventures in Online Dating. Constance lives in Asheville, NC. Please visit her at www.constancelombardo.com

Giving Characters Agency in Restricted Situations

LYN MILLER-LACHMANN

In the past, I've written about Passive Protagonist Syndrome, a reason many manuscripts never see the light of day—or often enough, the words "THE END." Basically, Passive Protagonist Syndrome occurs when the main character is primarily an observer without taking action to drive the story forward. Taking action can affect the world around the protagonist, or it can change the protagonist's own situation and relationships with others in their life. Action does not have to be earth-shattering to make for a good story.

By their very nature, children's books—especially those for very young children—face a challenge. The younger the child, the more limited their world, and the greater their dependence on adults to make consequential decisions and to follow through on those decisions. That's one reason why many picture books feature animals or inanimate objects as protagonists. For instance, a bear—even (or especially) a childlike bear such as the one in my friend Sandra Nickel's duology *Big Bear and Little Fish* and *Bear's Big Idea*—can live on its own and go on adventures in a way that a six-year-old child can't. I faced this challenge in writing my own picture book, *Ways to Play*, which features a human protagonist on the autism spectrum. *Ways to Play* draws textual and visual inspiration from the world of *Peanuts*, where adults are absent and kids attempt to solve their own problems with varying levels of success.

In writing my novels for teens, I faced a very different kind of challenge. All four of my YA novels feature teenagers growing up under dictatorships or living with the trauma from dictatorship. In general, teenagers are experiencing a wider world, in the process of separating from their parents and finding their place within their peer group and the wider society. But when teenagers grow up under dictatorship, their agency is far more limited.

Perhaps the adults in charge have forced them to move far from home for safety, the situation faced by Daniel and Tina in *Gringolandia* and its sequel, *Surviving Santiago*—novels set during the Pinochet dictatorship in Chile. If the teenagers remain inside their repressive countries, they may not be able to choose their profession or whether to continue their education. At the beginning of *Torch*, set in communist Czechoslovakia in 1969, readers learn that Pavol has been denied admission to university and ordered to report to work as a coal miner after graduating from high school. Even though he's worked hard and received top grades, his participation in a protest has led to this punishment. And in *Eyes Open*, set during Portugal's fascist dictatorship, Sónia's possibilities in life have been limited from the moment of her birth by the fact that she is a girl and not from a family in her country's ruling elite.

By their very nature, dictatorships infantilize the people who live under them. The ruler, or ruling party, monitors their private behavior and communications, censors a wide range of media and ideas, and enacts and strictly enforces laws for what the individual can and can't do, including requiring official permissions to travel both within the country and abroad. The "adventures" that my characters in *Torch* embark on in the course of the novel are, in fact, prohibited. They are real-life runaway bunnies.

So how to give agency to teens living in these very restricted circumstances, where the government deliberately makes people passive in order to control them more easily? For me, it was a trial-and-error process because I wrote another YA manuscript before *Eyes Open*, also set in Portugal during the Salazar dictatorship but featuring a different protagonist who failed to overcome Passive Protagonist Syndrome. If you've read the verse novel, you may have caught the cameo appearance of Rosália, one of the older sisters of Sónia's rebellious boyfriend. Although she tried to keep her younger brother out of trouble, Rosália was primarily a narrator of other characters' struggles, including those of poetry-writing Sónia of whose actions she strongly disapproved. While most of the girls, including Rosália, chafe against their restricted lives, Sónia struggles the most. At first, her actions consist of writing poetry to honor her boyfriend in prison and trying to identify the snitches who landed him there and later cost her extended family the restaurant that had been their livelihood for three generations. But as she toils in a hotel laundry after being forced to drop out of school, she learns both the power and the price of taking real action against the regime and its many surrogates.

Does Sónia change the world? Does she bring down the dictatorship like Katniss in the *Hunger Games* trilogy? No, and that wouldn't be accurate at the time this novel is set (which is why historical novels set in dictatorships tend to take place near the end of those regimes). But there are ways of showing character agency even if the protagonist doesn't change the world. Maybe they save the life of a friend, or obtain a small concession that turns out to have greater impact later on. Or if they can't bring freedom to their country, they can find freedom for themselves. Maybe, even if evil wins, the protagonist lives to fight another day, and at the end of a harrowing adventure, that's all the reader can hope for.

Lyn Miller-Lachmann
New York City, December 2024

LYN MILLER-LACHMANN is the author of the YA historical novel Torch, winner of the 2023 Los Angeles Times Book Prize for Young Adult Literature, and the YA verse novel Eyes Open, chosen by Booklist as a Top 10 Historical Fiction for Youth, 2024. She wrote the picture book *Ways to Play* and co-authored with Zetta Elliott the middle grade verse novel *Moonwalking*. Her nonfiction includes a biography of Temple Grandin in the *She Persisted* chapter book series and *Film Makers: 15 Groundbreaking Women Directors*, co-authored with Tanisia "Tee" Moore. Lyn translates books for youth from Portuguese to English, including the 2023 YA graphic novel *Pardalita* by Joana Estrela, a 2024 Batchelder Honor Book, and the YA graphic novel *Our Beautiful Darkness*, by the Angolan author Ondjaki, illustrated by António Jorge Gonçalves, a Kirkus Best Book of 2024. Find her and her activities (including a LEGO city called Little Brick Township) at lynmillerlachmann.com.

What Climate Fiction Can Teach Us About Hope

GLORIA MUÑOZ

This fall, my city was affected by two back-to-back hurricanes. I live in a Southern coastal region where every hurricane and record-breaking heat wave pushes us closer to the undeniable urgency of climate change and to the irreversible long-term effects of sea-level rise in coastal regions. Each day a different species inches closer towards extinction. The fires, the floods, hurricanes, tornadoes, and earthquakes—all have somehow become staples in the headlines. I want my debut novel, *This Is the Year,* to remain fiction, but like science fiction, climate fiction can feel prophetic, if not cautionary.

Climate narratives are a part of our zeitgeist. And to put it plainly, climate change is overwhelming. But we depend on the health of our planet, so there is no looking away. *This Is the Year* is a hybrid cli-fi (climate fiction) novel that considers how we hold onto hope in the face of the climate crisis. When writing it, I knew I'd have to strike a balance between the bleak and difficult realities of the state of our planet and the community building, levity, and even humor that intersect our lives during challenging times.

This is not an easy task. The helplessness of our environmental disaster cannot be sugarcoated by heroic arcs or happy endings. But YA fiction—which is typically about navigating internal and external challenges with the help of friends and community—is the perfect place to carry out an honest dialogue about climate change. Teens today were born into a mess, but they are also some of the most outspoken, creative, humorous, and innovative minds we have today. I wrote *This Is the Year* for them because I believe that young people have the capacity, prudence, and hope to enact change.

Teens will continue to be teens even when the world feels like it's ending. The characters in *This Is the Year* were developed with this in mind. They have their own passions and frustrations. Juli, the protagonist, and Jeanine, her nemesis, forced to work an intimidating amount of volunteer hours, are faced with the grim impacts of climate change as they clean beaches and help track shorebirds. Although the two start as enemies, they find a common ground through their work (and mutual love of roller skating). Mari, the resident theater kid, imagines a potentially hopeful future through plays and in the planning and décor of a school dance. Roger, who plays the cello and lives with his Sony's on his head, finds and helps care for a bird that crashed into a building's window. From my lived experience and in my research for *This Is the Year*, I have found that issues of climate change are often interlaced with the everyday. While each character is affected by the repercussions of climate change in some way, they all have big dreams and hopes for their futures as well. On the brink of graduation, they have the rest of their lives ahead of them *if* and only *if* they can take action and imagine a different world.

In *This Is the Year*, as in our reality, high rises and developers continue to buy land and disenfranchise and displace communities. This discord has become more prevalent in the shadow of the pandemic. As Penn State meteorologist Gregory Jenkins told *The Washington Post*, "Racism is 'inexorably' linked to climate change because it dictates who benefits from activities that produce planet-warming gases and who suffer most from the consequences." While people of color are disproportionately more affected by the ramifications of climate change, their voices and concerns are not always at the forefront of these policy-making conversations. What can we do when profit is put before people? At its core, *This Is the Year* asks, "What voices are not invited to the table when we build future cities?" And, "How have immigrants been writing environmental futures all along?" I hope my work helps expand the dialogue of cli-fi with an eye for inclusivity.

As a novelist, poet, translator, and daughter of Colombian immigrants, I'm particularly motivated to highlight migrant, undocumented, first generation, Southern narratives. *This Is the Year* engages with how people relate to ever-shifting environments and imagine futures in the wake of this human-caused ecological crisis. I hope the novel, which combines forms (prose and verse), exists beyond its published form to spark ideas in classrooms and communities, and serves as a roadmap for how to hold onto joy and hope in the face of oppression, grief, and environmental loss.

After a hurricane, destruction and beauty coexist. People's lives are turned upside down, homes are damaged, trees fallen, nothing looks the same. In that same aftermath, people show up for one another in big and small ways. Neighbors help clear our homes, cut tree branches, feed one another. A very large oak tree fell on my home during Hurricane Milton. We had a mountain of debris outside of our home for months. Kids in the neighborhood drew smiley faces on the rounds of cut trees. This small gesture made staring at the destruction a little less devastating. On our walks around the neighborhood, we found smiley faces spray-painted on nearly every pile of debris. Hope finds its way back into our lives even, and perhaps especially, in the dark times.

The characters in the novel show up for each other repeatedly, even when Juli, who is struggling with personal grief, tries to push everyone away. *This Is the Year* is a book that asks hard questions and invites readers to be open to using their wit, creativity, and hope to help Juli make sense of the world. We need young adult fiction that makes room for the grief and hope of the climate crisis. These works will be the guides that help teach us how to observe, reach forward, traverse new borders, and, perhaps more poignantly, how to revel in and show up for the people, animals, and places we love.

GLORIA MUÑOZ is a Colombian American writer and advocate for multilingual literacy who enjoys writing about plants, migrations, star stuff, and the environments that shape us. She is the author of the poetry collections, *Your Biome Has Found You* and *Danzirly*, which won the Ambroggio Prize and the Florida Gold Medal Book Award for Poetry. She is an Academy of American Poets Poet Laureate Fellow, a Hedgebrook Fellow, a Macondista, a member of Las Musas, and a Highlights Foundation Diverse Verse Fellow. *This Is the Year* is her debut novel. Visit Gloria on social media at @bygloriamunoz and on her website at gloriamunoz.com.

Look at What I'da Missed

DR. CHEA PARTON

On any given day, whenever I'm facing a problem—big or small—I hear various catch phrases from the older generations of my family that help to buoy and propel me to persevere. My mom's parents (Mamaw and Papaw) grew up in rural Indiana with very little and worked hard and managed to achieve a mostly middle-class existence. My Appalachian grandparents moved from rural East Tennessee to rural Indiana because they were starving and had a line on some farm work but never managed to achieve middle-class status.

My dad was working chicken houses as a fourth-grader to help support the family, and my mom worked the corn fields as a seventh-grader to start paying some of her own way—a tradition that I reluctantly carried on in my own teenage years.

We were a story-telling family on all sides. Supper

time was story hour as were the many campfires anticipating and celebrating cool autumn nights. Each word settling in my bones, nourishing and strengthening for a life they knew full well was bursting with both joy and struggle. And those stories seem to surface in moments where I really need them, especially as a farm kid in higher education.

**

"Mama, what is a 'registrar'?" I asked close to tears. "I keep getting these orange notices in my mailbox. They seem serious, but I have no idea what they mean."

"It's a building on campus, Sis. Get your campus map, find it, and go ask them." I could hear the chaos in the background. There were still four kids at home and I knew she was probably hurting without my help. "I'm not gonna be here forever. Only one who will always take care of you is you. Now, I gotta go. Love you."

I felt so stupid. Like it was something I should've known but didn't. What good is it to have a parent who went to college if they weren't willing to help you navigate it? Even though I was the first person in my dad's family to graduate from college, I wasn't technically first-gen, so didn't qualify for any of those supports. I was just a kid from a town with the population of her dorm, trying to figure out how to exist in a place that didn't seem like it was meant for me.

I read those orange papers probably close to a hundred times trying to figure out what they meant. I knew enough to know I was beat and needed to go ask somebody. So, I did what she said. I looked up the building on the campus map and made my way over there. Thought briefly about using the bus system and then decided I felt stupid enough already and that would be just salt on my wound.

Walking in the door I heard my Papaw. "Ain't no shame in asking questions, Punk. Takes courage to admit what you don't know. How else are you gonna learn anything?"

So, I asked the question. Which I immediately regretted because I owed some money that I had to figure out how to pay. Or maybe not? They were just waiting on loan and scholarship money? I still didn't quite understand, and I tried not to feel ashamed about it the whole time.

**

"Every day's shit, Punk; some day's just a bigger pile." Today was definitely a bigger pile. I was barely making rent while working to get my teacher's license post-baccalaureate. I had already taken out more money than I wanted to in loans and was waiting tables and bartending at a restaurant that was clearly circling the drain when my mom called. I took it out on the loading dock, letting my legs dangle and swing off the side while the sun warmed my upturned face.

"So, I've been thinkin' it's time for you to start paying your car insurance." My mom's voice was clear and strong. Her mind clearly made up. It was one of the only expenses of mine she shouldered through my undergrad degree.

"But, Mama, I'm barely making rent."

"Guess you better get a second job, then. You'll figure it out."

The tears started as soon as she hung up. How the hell was I supposed to just up and get a second job? I had coursework to do on top of all this working. I started feeling sorry for myself, thinking about how if were any of my other siblings, my mom would've paid their way until they were dead.

"I can't do this."

"Can't never did nothin' for nobody," came the reply in my head.

So, I wiped my tears with the back of my hand. Made my way inside where I had a new table waiting for me, a two-top alighted by an older couple. I did all the things I knew I should do—worked hard to get them what they needed; helped other servers when they needed it; and was kind.

At some point the man, Lloyd, mentioned my work ethic and said he was looking for some help in a mail room on campus.

"As luck would have it, I'm on the market for a second job," I said with a smile.

He invited me down for an interview and hired me on the spot. Maybe the shit-pile wasn't as big as I thought it was after all.

**

My first year of doctoral work, I failed my first

review because I was a cooperative overlapper (someone who talks alongside and at times on top of another's words to build conversation) and no one thought to ask me why I participated the way I did. It was an urban-located and urban-focused program. There were only two rural-identifying people in my cohort, and one of them was me. Worried that a seemingly middle-class, white woman was taking up too much talk time from other folks, my professors chastised me by demanding that I write a paper about how I would no longer participate in a way that helped me to learn best in order to continue to stay in the program.

I was hurt and madder'n a wet hen. I wanted to quit. But I was in a state thousands of miles away from home on a full fellowship and couldn't see how giving in was an option. I was the first person on both sides of the family to work on a doctoral degree and once again in uncomfortable and uncharted waters.

I sat down to write that stupid paper, about how I wouldn't use the tools I was socialized to have to build knowledge and ideas through conversation; about how I wouldn't intimidate other people into silence and I heard Uncle Leroy: "You go inside and be grateful to be inside, and then you come outside and be grateful to be out."

We were talking about factory work and how much he hated it but was grateful for it because it allowed him to provide for his family in a way he never would have if they would've stayed in Appalachia. He once fist-fought my grandpa for a bit of cornbread they found while sweeping the dirt floor of their hand-hewn shack, even though neither of them new how old or edible it was.

So, I kept typing the words, grateful for the opportunity to write them; for the sustained upward mobility that my family had literally fought for.

**

All of these stories about where we started have helped me overcome the obstacles and hiccups I've experienced inside and outside of my academic journey. When a piece I worked tirelessly to write as an advocate of rural students and teachers was rejected from a journal; when university after university decided not to hire me; when the rural education consulting business I tried to build didn't take off; I remember the countless ways my elders showed me how to survive.

Grandpa Adam more than once saved his own life. One time by learning how to swim after his daddy threw him off his shoulders in a raging river so that at least one of them would survive. Another time by pressing down on his neck so hard he staunched the bleeding caused by a bucking chainsaw while he was clearing a fence row. He was in the tree and had to climb down one handed. He was 71 years old.

Papaw lost his leg to a corn head while walking rows during harvest. My cousin was driving the combine and they miscommunicated about where Papaw was going to be. He was life-lined by helicopter to a hospital where he had eight surgeries in seven days to try to save his leg. But when he developed an infection, he told them to "cut it off and throw it away." That was November of his 71st year. In February he was up on a ladder clearing leaves off the roof and out of the gutters.

About ten years after he lost his leg, I was talking with Papaw as my kids, his great-grands, wreaked havoc in my mom's kitchen. He was wearing his sideways grin, most certainly enjoying the ornery and lively energy the kids brought to the house. I asked him something that I'd wondered for a while—if he ever wished he'd gone out in the field with his boots on. Since the accident he'd developed a Parkinson's-like syndrome and struggled to do many of the things he still wanted to be able to do. "Hell, no, Punk!" he said, sweeping his arm through the air as if he were gathering each of us. "Look at all I'da missed."

I have no way of knowing what will come for me in my own 71st year or the years leading up to it, but I know that I will have what it takes to make it through because my elders have shown me how. Survival is never perfect and rarely is it pretty, but it can be done with gratitude and contentment. If they could do it, I can too, and I'll persevere as best I can 'cause I don't wanna miss nothin'.

DR. CHEA PARTON grew up on a farm and still considers herself a farm girl. She is currently a rural middle school teacher and begins every day with her students in a barn feeding animals and cleaning stalls. She also works with pre-service teachers as an instructor at Purdue University. She is passionate about rural education. Her research focuses on the personal and professional identity of rural and rural out-migrant teachers as well as rural representation in YA literature. She wrote <u>Country Teachers in City Schools: The Challenge of Negotiating Identity and Place</u> and a number *of journal publications. She currently runs Literacy In Place where she seeks to catalogue rural YA books and provide teaching resources. She also hosts the Reading Rural YAL podcast where she gives book talks and interviews rural YA authors. You can reach her at readingrural@gmail.com.*

Don't Fear the Spoon:
Thoughts on Quitting Your Day Job

SEAN PETRIE

"There is no path." Ethan Hawke, on a creative life
"There is no spoon." That kid in The Matrix

At a book release I went to a few months ago, author Jennifer Mathieu was asked, "What's your best advice for writers who are starting out?"

"Don't quit your day job," she replied.

I sat up in my chair. I've been a creative writer, making up stories and poems, for over two decades. I make some money through my creative work, but not a ton. For the bulk of my income, I rely on my "day job" as a law professor. And, at least once a year, I ask myself:

Should I quit that job and go all-in on creative?

It's a dilemma I think nearly every writer struggles with, unless you are lucky enough to come out of the gates with a bestseller or have a partner/parent who can support you until you become financially successful.

Mathieu, a successful author by any measure, went on to describe how her day job gave her the financial stability to write to her passion, rather than to her pocket book. (She didn't use that phrase, I just made it up.) She also said her particular day job—a high school English teacher—also allowed her the time to write, especially during the summers.

For many creatives navigating their professional path, those tie into what I consider The Big Three questions:

> 1. Money: If I quit my day job, can I make enough to eat, pay rent, maybe buy that fancy purple shirt? Will I still be able to write what I *want*?
> 2. Time: If I quit and go all-in creatively, how much more writing could I do? How much *would* I do?
> 3. Self-Worth: Am I even good enough to try? (Oh hey there, Imposter Syndrome.)

Will this essay answer all those for you? *Absolutely!*

It will also teach you how to write an instant bestseller, understand cryptocurrency, and throw a wicked split-finger fastball.

If only.

But here's what this essay *will* do: In the next few pages, I'll share what I've discovered about the creative path—what's worked and not worked, for me and some of my writer friends. Because one of the best ways to learn is from stories, right?

The first time I quit my day job

About twenty years ago, I was semi-fresh out of law school, working as a full-time attorney at a big law firm. But I was antsy. So I took a soul-searching road trip, during which I decided I wanted to write books. For kids.

Why children's books? Well, growing up I'd always been creative (drawing, writing Shel-Silverstein-like poems, cracking jokes in class) and a huge reader. And in my late twenties, I continued to be drawn to books for kids. A big reason was Ellen Raskin's *The Westing Game*. I first read that book in fifth grade, as we drove across the country to move from Ohio to Texas, just after my mom had remarried. The more I read, the more I identified with *The Westing Game*'s main character, Turtle Wexler—like her, I was moving to a new place and felt like nobody really understood me. I found some comfort in those pages, in her story.

Fast-forward to me at age 28, on that soul-searching road trip. (Sidenote: As I am typing this, I'm realizing that 28-year-old-me was paralleling fifth-grade-me, traveling across the county on a new path. Except I was driving the opposite route, *from* Texas to Ohio. Which I'm sure has some deeper meaning…that I won't explore here!) Anyway, on my drive, I stopped at the Cooperative Children's Book Center (CCBC) in Madison, Wisconsin, where I chatted with the woman at the front desk, Ginny Moore Kruse. When I mentioned *The Westing Game*, Ginny's face lit up. Turned out she and Ellen Raskin had been good friends, and hey, would I like to see Ellen's original papers and some videos, all of which were housed at the CCBC?

Um, yes please.

I spent the next several hours in a CCBC side room immersed in all things Raskin. And when I finished, I knew: *This* is what I want to do—I want to write books like Ellen Raskin did, but in my own voice. Books that can maybe speak to one kid, make them laugh, or thrill with the challenge of solving a mystery, or be a companion in a scary situation like moving across the country. So, for me, the passion was there.

Which I think is incredibly important to identify for any creative, right from the start: *Why do you want to do this thing, this creative work? How badly?*

For me, the idea of writing books for kids made me perk up. Like in the TV show *The Big Bang Theory*, when someone says "Sheldon Cooper," and Sheldon replies: "That's *Doctor* Sheldon Cooper." His shoulders go up and back, and he smiles proudly. (Try it.) That's how writing for kids has made me feel from day one: "I write *books*. For *kids*."

On the flip side, my job practicing law, for the most part, made me slump. Or, as a good lawyer friend put it: "It made you grayer. Not in age or hair but in spark."

So I saved up enough money to last a year. And then, when I turned 30, I celebrated by quitting my day job as an attorney to go all-in on writing books for kids. I hit send on the email to my law firm, then yelled FREEDOM! in my best *Braveheart* voice.

The same day, I wrote my friends and colleagues, announcing my grand start. Several of them, including the judge I had clerked for, said things like, "No, seriously—what do you *really* plan to do?" Friends would call me during the week and ask me to meet them out. "I can't," I would reply, "I'm working on my book." "Oh come on, you're just writing!" (Ah, the power of the word *just*.)

Which brings me to one of the Big Three: self-worth. To even consider quitting your day job, you need to believe this creative thing is your calling. And that you are worth that calling.

At another recent book event, my good writer friend, Cynthia Leitich Smith, recounted that when she quit her law job at age 28 to go all-in on writing, her lawyer friends flew into town for an intervention. (Really.) It may not be that extreme, but if you quit your day job, your non-artist friends and family will almost certainly question your choice. They may even treat it like (just) a hobby.

To go all-in, you need that passion, that drive, that pretty darn strong inside voice saying that if you *don't* quit your day job, you'll be selling out. You'll need that voice in the face of adversity. Even from friends. Maybe especially from them.

When I quit my day job at 30, I was lucky enough to have two of the Big Three: self-worth, and enough money to last a year. Where I didn't do so well was the other one: time.

Soon after I quit, I bought a miniature library of creative-writing craft books. (I certainly would have bought *this* book if it had existed!) I also bought tons of kids books, to see what was selling and winning awards. I went to seminars and even flew out to LA for the Society of Children's Book Writers & Illustrators national conference.

And in the first few months, I wrote an entire picture book. It was called *This Class Is a Zoo!* and I sent it directly to editors I'd met at the national conference, one of whom at Henry Holt loved it, and sent it on to acquisitions.

I'd made it! Not even halfway into my year off!

A month later the acquisitions folks said no. I tried other editors, and then agents, no luck. So I put the zoo picture book aside and started a middle grade novel called *The Zoo Hunt* (I have a thing for zoos) loosely patterned after *The Westing Game*. I wrote a killer opening chapter.

Then, because I knew I'd need it for all the other pages I'd soon write, I bought a top-of-the-line laptop. Then, to print all those pages, I bought a nice laser printer. Then I upgraded to a color one to printout the cover, thinking hey, if a publisher doesn't bite in a few months, I could publish my own books. I looked into a small printing press and book-binding machines.

I also bought tons of office supplies, labeled folders with things like, "Agent Queries" and "Publisher Guidelines." I dusted every corner of my apartment. What I didn't do a whole lot of, for the rest of that year, was write.

Maybe that first rejection dented my self-worth; maybe I was scared everyone would say no to this zoo book, too. Or maybe I thought, "I still have half a year of money left!" Probably both. My apartment was spit-spot clean. But so were those printer pages.

So, if you quit your day job, you may *have* the time

to write, but you also need the discipline to *use* that time for actual writing. Maybe you already have that skillset—huzzah! At 30, I did not. But stick around—I've learned some ways to help.

That first year did not go exactly as I'd expected. But does life ever? So here's another thing I've learned. I'll amend the Big Three to add both a question and an observation:

> 4. Don't Fear the Spoon: What if your creative journey doesn't go as planned? (Pro tip: It won't.) At some point you'll come to a fork in the road. Sometimes it'll be so unexpected, it won't even be a fork. It'll be a spoon. Don't be afraid to take it.

Here's an example: I have a writer friend who, when he started out, was sure he'd write middle grade novels. Then, after a few years of struggling with that genre and keeping his day job, he stumbled across a picture book biography project. He tried it, and something immediately clicked. A year or so later, he quit his day job. He's still writing those picture book biographies (and other books) full time. I think he would say he's infinitely grateful he took that spoon.

For me, at least four spoons have popped up along my creative journey—four completely unexpected routes. I was afraid to take each one. But I'm so glad I did.

Spoon #1: Teaching

A year after quitting my attorney job, I ran out of

money. I didn't want to go back to the soul-sucking work of practicing law, but I needed to eat and pay rent. As I was looking into various law firms, a friend at the University of Texas reached out and said, "Hey, we have an opening to teach legal writing. You interested?"

Uh, maybe?

I liked the idea of teaching law instead of practicing it. And I figured it would give me more time to write than working at a firm. But a firm job was something I *knew* I could do. I'd never taught before. And working as an attorney would pay more. Way more. The teaching position wasn't full-time—it was as an adjunct, for one semester—and the pay would be $6,000 total, no benefits.

I took the teaching spoon.

That first semester was rough. I barely wrote anything creative; nearly all my time was spent developing lesson plans and grading. (As any teacher knows, grading is its own form of soul-sucking.) But other than the grading part, I loved it. I'd always liked public speaking, and being in the classroom, interacting with students, made me the opposite of "gray." Plus I was no longer writing briefs to defend companies I often didn't care about (and who were often in the wrong). Nope, now I was teaching others how to do that. But also teaching them to defend against legitimate injustices. (Which, goodness knows we need, today more than ever.)

At the end of the semester, a full-time teaching spot opened up. I took it.

The next year was even rougher. I was assigned to a different course, so I had to develop entirely new lesson plans. Which meant I did basically zero creative work. But I still loved my day job, and I now had a salary. True, it was a fraction of what I could have made as an attorney, but it came with health insurance and a retirement plan, and gave me enough money for food, rent, and an occasional purple-sparkly shirt.

My second year of full-time teaching was much better for my creative life. I got to teach the same class, so I could re-use the same lesson plans. Which freed up more time to write; not as much as when I'd quit my day job, but definitely more than when I was an attorney.

As my best friend and college roommate—and probably the smartest person my age that I know (he is not a writer)—said to me at the time, "For what you want to do, I really don't see a better balance than that: teaching and writing."

Taking the teaching spoon gave me a decent balance of creative time and steady income, in a day job I enjoyed. It also let me pursue something I'd long wanted—an MFA in writing.

In my third year of full-time teaching (still re-using those same lesson plans, yes!) I enrolled at the amazing Vermont College of Fine Arts (VCFA). I was able to do that while teaching full-time because VCFA had a distance program—we were on campus for two weeks in the summer and two in the winter, but the rest I did from Austin. (Teaching full-time also gave me the money to pay for it.) After two years, I got my MFA in Writing for Kids, and it was even better than I'd hoped in terms of friendships, craft, and the community of being on that gorgeous campus in Montpelier. But it also taught me something I hadn't expected:

While I was working full-time and doing the MFA program, I actually got *more* writing done than when I'd quit my day job.

Which I think is a key part of the creative journey: being open to what you learn about yourself on the way.

What I learned about myself was that I get more creative work done when I'm accountable to someone else. I've always been good at jumping through hoops. So—within reason—the more external deadlines I have, the more I seem to get done. I had less free time as a professor than when I'd quit my day job, but I *used* that time much better because I was responsible to someone else, at Vermont College. Maybe having unaccountable free time is a form of writer's block for me, akin to a boundless blank page.

In any event, I gained some valuable self-knowledge doing the MFA program—but it would take me a decade to remember it again, to realize how much I needed those external hoops in my creative life, and to figure out how to get them back. (Without getting another MFA.)

But in the meantime, the Vermont College program had given me another bonus: an agent.

While I was on campus, a big-time agent saw my writing and wanted to represent me. I was thrilled and of course signed on! But after a couple years we parted ways, when it became apparent that she was big-time mostly in adult romance, not kid lit. Which I didn't even think about when I signed on—I was starry-eyed at someone simply saying yes, the way Ferris Bueller described his best friend, Cameron: "He's going to marry the first person he sleeps with."

I don't regret signing with that agent. If anything, it boosted that all-important self-worth. But in the end, the road you're on, no matter how glittery it might seem, might not be leading where you want. Don't be afraid to step off it. And don't be surprised—or afraid—if another spoon pops up.

Spoon #2: Typewriters

Not long after my agent split, a friend asked me to be part of a creative experiment: to make up poems for people at a craft fair, on old typewriters. I was still a bit down from not having an agent, and I hadn't written a poem since elementary school. *There's no way I'm good enough to do something like that*, I thought. (Oh hey, welcome back, Imposter Syndrome.)

I alllllllmost told my friend "no thanks." But I got myself out of bed that morning and showed up. (Hello, external deadlines.) And I discovered not only was I able to write poems, I was able to write them on-the-spot, on a clackety old typewriter—and I was good at it. Darn good.

That spoon wasn't supposed to last more than a day. But people at the craft fair loved our typewriter experiment, and it snowballed into something that has been going strong for more than a decade. It's called Typewriter Rodeo, and it lets me type poems at events all over the country, teach poetry workshops, even perform radio poems on NPR. It led to my first published book, a collection of poems and stories co-written with the other Rodeo poets. And to my second agent.

So sometimes, when life gives you typewriters, make poems.

Typewriter Rodeo turned out better than I ever could have imagined—it let me do gigs like type at the Smithsonian Museum next to (but not *on*, please don't touch!) their old typewriters, and write a poem at the Sun Valley Writers Conference for Judy Blume (!). It also paid decent money. But not enough to quit my day job. To do that, I realized I would need *lots* of gigs, and lots of big-paying corporate-y ones, which sometimes aren't as fun as museums and writing festivals. In other words, to make the Rodeo work financially on its own, I knew I'd have to sell out—become the equivalent of a law-firm poet.

So I kept that balance: teaching, writing, Rodeoing. But the older I got, the stronger I felt the itch to go all-in creatively.

I kept telling myself, "Maybe next year…" Which is easier to do at age 35. But at 45, I started to realize hey, maybe I don't have forever. And so…

The second time I quit my day job
After ten years of teaching full-time, I went to the law school and said, "I need a year off." I didn't want to completely give up my day job, but I wanted more time to write. And if the law school said no, I was prepared to quit outright. But they didn't; instead they granted me a "Leave of Absence"—an unpaid year with my job guaranteed when (if) I came back.

Just like the first time I'd quit my day job, I'd saved up some money to get me through. But unlike before,

I bought zero printers. I went to zero writing seminars. Instead, I moved to Seattle (where my new agent was) and brought along the bare minimums: my trusty laptop, my favorite flannel, a warm rain jacket and waterproof boots. And of course my typewriter.

Then, between long walks in the misty rain and meals at the local pub, I wrote.

I worked on a middle grade novel that was calling to me (about a kid who writes poems on a typewriter). A friend asked if I was interested in doing work-for-hire projects. I'd never considered it before, but I took that detour and ended up writing six short kids' books that only paid two months of rent, but were a blast because I got to choose the topics. I also set up my typewriter each week at the local West Seattle farmers market, writing poems for tips. Through that, I got a book of my poems published by the local historical society, who included photos to go along with each poem. I made zero money on that book, but dang it's gorgeous.

When my "Leave of Absence" was up, I had a handful of books in the world that I was (and still am) really proud of. But I had less than a handful of money left.

So I went back to my day job of teaching law. That was five years ago. Since then, I've taken two very important spoons.

Spoon #3: Burlwood

The first time I quit my day job, I toyed with the idea of self-publishing. But I never considered publishing anyone *else's* books. A couple years ago, that changed.

(Trigger warning: sad story in the next paragraph.)

In 2022, I invited a young Austin poet, Erika Evans, to be part of Typewriter Rodeo. A month before her first gig with us, she was tragically killed. I met with Erika's dad shortly after, and he said he wished there was some way for her poems and art, which had never been published, to be shared with the world.

"I could try," I said.

And so I collected Erika's poetry and artwork, made it into a book, and then published it using a print-on-demand model. I did that solely as a favor to her family. (You can read more about that project in the "About Burlwood" section at the end of this book.)

A few months later, a poet friend said to me: "Hey, I have this idea for a book, but I don't know how to get it published..."

I considered telling my friend, "Yeah it's tough out there—good luck!" Publishing Erika's book had taken a ton of time. And wasn't cheap. Doing another book would similarly eat into my own creative time and my savings. But putting together a book for someone else, making it exist in the world, had sparked something in me. It was a lot of work, but it made me the opposite of gray.

I sat up in my chair. "I think I could make that happen," I told my poet friend.

So I hired a cover designer, a copyeditor, and a marketing person, and Burlwood Books was born. There is simply no way I could have done that without the money from my day job.

As a publisher of other people's work, I don't make

any income (quite the opposite), but I do get to help people's creative dreams become real, and make beautiful books exist. Like this one. Which might never have happened, if it hadn't been for my most recent spoon.

Spoon #4: Accountability

Way back when I first started writing, I joined a critique group. We would meet every so often, exchange a chapter (or not), and talk about our writing. Those were wonderful, but not always the most productive in terms of getting words on the page.

Eventually, I started meeting for writing times with one or two close friends ("swim buddies," as Jennifer Richard Jacobson calls them in her essay in this book). We wouldn't critique each other's work. Instead we'd meet, sit next to each other, and write. (I'm doing that right now in fact, beside my closest writing friend, Rebecca Bendheim.) A year ago, during one of our writing times, Rebecca turned to me on a break and said, "I hired an accountability coach."

"A what?"

She explained how she met with her coach each Monday (via Zoom) to set goals for the week, then on Friday she emailed her coach a progress report with attachments. Her coach didn't read any of the attachments, just offered encouragement or advice, and probably most important, was simply *there* each week.

"Kind of like us," I replied, "meeting to write."

"Exactly. Only I pay her."

I was skeptical. I didn't think it would be useful if the other person didn't give me any feedback. Why would I pay someone basically to receive my emails and be a cheerleader? Wouldn't that be a waste of money, and wouldn't the weekly meetings and reports eat into my already-limited free time?

But I trusted Rebecca. So I took that spoon and hired an accountability coach. It's been a game-changer.

In the last year, I've written and revised an entire middle grade novel, put together a book of kids poems by the Typewriter Rodeo poets (look for it soon!), along with two other books for my publishing company—a gorgeous tarot therapy guide by a Seattle therapist, and the amazing collection of essays currently in your hands. I was still teaching full-time, but over the past year I got more creative work done than ever.

Which shouldn't have surprised me—I'd done the same thing when I'd had the accountability of my MFA program. Only now, I had an actual accountability coach. I also had the accountability of my regular writing times with friends like Rebecca. (I almost had that even earlier: In December 2019, my writing friend Christina Soontornvat leased a cubicle in a co-working space and I leased the one beside her, and we planned to "go to the office" a few times a week to write. Then, alas, covid hit.)

It took me ten years to *re*-realize it, but having regularity and responsibility—to someone else—lets me get more done, even with a day job. And, as Jennifer Mathieu said in her talk, having the day job has let me not worry about writing for money—I've had the freedom to work on projects that I love. I'm so incredibly proud of my books that exist in the world. To me, that is worth way more than a closet full of sparkly-purple shirts.

Could I have written *more* if I hadn't been teaching? Of course.

Well, at least I could have for little while, until my savings said otherwise. And maybe that little while is all I'd need—to get a big book deal, then more school visits, then a bigger deal, etc. Maybe that's what's next…

Now what?

Are there times that I regret not having quit my day job for good? Sure. But there is also the small shelf of my own books that I'm so proud of, that I didn't have to sell-out to write. And the growing shelf of books I've helped create for others. For me, that's a darn good tradeoff.

But that's "for me."

Your creative journey is just that—yours. Ask yourself, is the passion there? *Why* do you want to do this creative thing so badly? Maybe take a soul-searching road trip to find out. Or a walk around the block. Maybe you already know.

For me, there's a reason that Jennifer Mathieu's comment made me sit up in my seat a few months ago. Maybe I'm getting close to quitting my day job for good. Does the idea of doing that make *you* sit up?

Maybe you will go all-in sooner than me. Or later. As F. Scott Fitzgerald said, "It's never too late to be whoever you want to be." Or maybe your current day job already gives you the ideal money-creative balance. Maybe you really want that fancy purple shirt, or need the money for something much more important.

Everyone's path is different—which is another way of saying there is no path. Looking back, there have been lots of milestones on my journey: abandoned printers and well-used typewriters, unfinished zoo manuscripts and published books, along with thousands of poems. But there's still a lot more ahead.

As I type this sentence, I'm in a coffeehouse in Austin sitting beside my writing friend Rebecca. In a few months, she is quitting her day job (the second time for her), to go all-in on creative. Maybe I'll join her. Just this week, I taped a small piece of paper on my computer that reads, "If not now, when?"

Remember, there is no path.

So hey, go make yours. And along the way, take a spoon or two.

Sean Petrie
Austin, TX
February 2025

SEAN PETRIE *is an award-winning author, poet, and professor. He is also a co-founder of the nationally-acclaimed Typewriter Rodeo poetry troupe, and founder of Burlwood Books. His books include the* Jett Ryder *adventure-history series for kids (JollyFish Press),* Typewriter Rodeo: Real People, Real Stories, Custom Poems *(Andrews McMeel), the IPPY-award winning* Listen to the Trees: A Poetic Snapshot of West Seattle, Then & Now *(Documentary Media), and the Moonbeam Children's Award-winning* Pet Poems (also not just pets) *collection of illustrated poems and companion workbook.*

Sean teaches poetry workshops across the country, and is also a legal writing professor at The University of Texas School of Law. He has a law degree from Stanford and an MFA in Writing for Kids from the Vermont College of Fine Arts. Sean lives in Austin with his dog, Margo, and owns way too many typewriters. Please visit him at www.seanpetrie.com

Layering in the Details That Matter

BETH REVIS

You may have heard that there are no new ideas under the sun, and that can sound *horrible* to someone trying to write a unique book. What do you mean my totally unique idea was already used by Shakespeare or Aristotle or *The Simpsons*?

But the reality is…it's true. There's a version of your absolutely mind-boggling twist written by Agatha Christie already. There are hints of your star-crossed enemies-to-lovers story in folklore and mythology. There are archetypes and hero's journeys and tropes and nothing is new, nothing at all.

Except the *way* you write it.

A novel is not a list of events. It's not emotionless dialogue presented as a script. What makes a novel its own unique form of art is the way you, the writer, use prose to develop a new perspective on all those old ideas that recycle through the centuries.

And the first way we do that is through description.

Layering in the point of view of your character—which is unique, even in a retelling or historical fiction—naturally makes your story stand out. And if you can layer that into your descriptions on a prose level, not merely in the voice of the character, you elevate your work into art.

Before I dive into that, though, a few definitions:

1. **Physical Description:** What the narrating character sees
2. **Emotional Description:** What the narrating character feels internally
3. **Sensory Description:** Going beyond visual, what does the narrating character feel, hear, smell, taste?
4. **Relative Description:** Linking the descriptions to something relevant to the plot or character development

To give you a few examples of this in action:

1. **Physical Description:** Shadows stretched long in the house on the third week without power.
2. **Emotional Description:** Seeing them, all I could think about was how grateful I was that our biggest losses involved modern-day luxuries like working lights, flushing toilets, and cell phone signals, losses we would easily recover from, unlike those who had been near the rivers and lakes.

3. **Sensory Description:** The silence permeated the house. The usual hum of the refrigerator, the beeps from my son's video games, and even the crackly voice of radio news were simply gone, echoing in emptiness.
4. **Relative Description:** All the silence was inside the house, but there was a cacophony outside that haunted our dreams: first, from the winds of the storm. Then from the alarms of emergency vehicles. And later, the constant sounds of chainsaws interrupting the confused birdsong. The world was in reverse, silence within, screaming without, all of it wrapped in impermeable darkness, our carefully caffeinated world now, once again, dictated by the sun.

I hope you can see from these different examples that all of this is describing something, but they each grow increasingly complex and more specific to the story. I could also have shifted the focus of the description:

> *Shadows stretched long in the house on the third week without power. It feels like a safe cocoon, the lack of air conditioning wrapping the humid air around our bodies like a blanket. I let the silence hold us. Perhaps it was cowardice or perhaps it was simply survival to be grateful for the downed trees that trapped us on our street, myopically condensing our worldview into shadows that hid the catastrophic destruction that changed the courses of the rivers, changed the courses of our neighbors' lives.*

These two different descriptions of life in the immediate aftermath of Hurricane Helene both draw out different images and—what's more—different meanings. One is focused on the duality of life and death, destruction and aid, and it's more distantly-focused, but confronting the reality of the situation even in the contrary descriptions. The other is smaller in scope, reflecting on the interior alone, a delay of facing the truth while cherishing the walls the held through the storm.

Notice that I kept the exact same line of physical description for both—and there's a reason for that.

Most beginning authors stop at the physical description. And that takes away the voice of the narrative.

Your job as a writer isn't to just "paint the picture" of what's happening. You want to evoke the feeling of the reader experiencing the story alongside the narrator, and very, very often, how the narrator describes the items and events that happen is directly linked to the narrative voice. So, if you've ever had an issue with what the voice of the story is, consider looking closely at the description.

Don't stop at what is, essentially, a list of visual items in the scene. Instead, linking the description to the character's senses, emotions, and connections to the story and the world is what makes for descriptive writing that really shines.

But there's one more step: layering.

Because often, as writers, we have to pause and think about the setting and consciously add in description, the tendency is to stop the narrative and dump a paragraph of description in whenever it occurs to us. Maybe the character goes into another room, and you recall that you need to describe it. Maybe the character starts to interact with an object that hasn't yet been seen.

My point is—don't *just* write the descriptive paragraph. Instead, layer it in with the action. Look through your manuscript and spot places where you have a chunk that's ultimately little more than description—then break it up, putting the different elements in among dialogue and action (remembering, of course, that action can literally just be walking down the street—a conversation while walking is more active than a convo while sitting unless you add tension somehow).

Add in what your character *does* and *why* with these descriptions that all link back to the narrator's unique perspective. This will carry you from plot point A to plot point B…but it will also make the reader realize what kind of person your character is, what they notice and care about, and what they dismiss. If, in the first example, the narrator left their house to help the people clearing the roads, all while thinking those descriptive thoughts, then you know that person is someone who doesn't just observe, but who also acts—much like all the first responders and heroes who came from all over the world to help the hurricane victims. And if you add in the narrator of the second description checking on her family, hugging her children, and then doing her best to contact family and friends out of her home, you'll know that this person cares about their loved ones and has an instinct to protect them and keep them safe.

Neither is wrong, but both are different.

Just like there's no new stories to be told, except in the way we tell them.

And while the story of Hurricane Helene is one of tragedy and death and innumerable loss, it's also one of hope, and resilience, and community.

It's all in how we tell the stories.

Beth Revis, January 7, 2025
Rutherford County, NC

BETH REVIS is an internationally acclaimed bestselling author with books available in more than 20 languages and has toured internationally to meet her fans. Five of her novels have listed in the NY Times. Beth primarily writes science fiction and fantasy for both adults and young adults. She's written three books for Star Wars, including the fan-beloved The Princess and the Scoundrel. Her most recent books include the historical romantasy duology starting with Night of the Witch, co-written with Sara Raasch, and a snarky sci fi novella series called Chaotic Orbits.

Beth is the co-owner of Wordsmith Workshops and the author of the Paper Hearts series, both of which aid aspiring authors. A native of North Carolina, Beth is currently working on multiple books. She lives in rural NC with her son, husband, and dog. You can find her at bethrevis.com.

How I Survive a Monolithic Life

JESS RINKER

Monolithic:

Dictionary:
-very large, united, and difficult to change

Me:
Sometimes life is just too big.

This is a truth you can count on: Life gives us more questions than answers. So many events have shaped me, both globally and in my own small life, and all have created hard-to-answer questions. Sometimes I've folded like warm, well-worked clay, and sometimes I've resisted, like a hot coal that just. Won't. Go. Out. From September 11th to the pandemic to my husband's stage four cancer diagnosis to war, war, war and in between, so much more. And that's not even diving into childhood traumas. Sometimes, it all seems too big for us adults, and since I'm a children's book author, and a mom, I'm always imagining what it's like for our young people to wrestle with these events and questions. For a ten-year old, a year is a significant amount of time, whereas, for this nearly fifty-year old, even a decade seems to speed by. How do children process these giant events without having as much experience in getting through to the other side? How do they stay resilient? How do they accept answers or lack thereof?

Back in 2020, when Covid first entered our lives, we were thrown into a global state of questioning. So many of the questions and issues that arose during the pandemic were the impetus of my most recent children's book, *Monolith*. The book isn't about a pandemic, rather how to handle huge questions and answers we may not want to accept. It's also a tangible, published example of the impetus of all of my writing—the processing of questions, answers, and life in general. Writing is the first way I think about anything, how I arrive at answers and how I accept I may not get them. But these days, it seems like we want answers, we want them fast, and we want them easy.

What's really stood out the most to me during the last five years of this desire to fast-track to the truth, is how people will *create answers* when they don't get the ones they want immediately. It's hard for humans to sit with uncertainty. Our brains tell us *unknowing* is a threat. I read one study where people who thought they might get an electric shock were actually more anxious than people who *knew* they were going to receive the shock. It's no wonder some organized religions provide absolutes and why conspiracy theorists get so much traction. Many of us don't want to accept that sometimes we simply don't get answers. For my part as an author, I want my readers to have assurance that we can be okay without those absolutes. We can still be good people, we can still work toward a common good, and still move forward, even if sometimes it feels like a centimeter at a time. If we give up, or sink into a cycle of conspiracy, or bulldoze those who don't agree, we go nowhere.

In 2018, my husband and I experienced a total loss from fire, which was caused by a truck crashing through an adjacent building. I had no idea it would become such a defining moment for me. Something so sudden, unexpected, and utterly destructive was incredibly hard to wrap my head around. I suddenly landed in a new, unfamiliar world where I didn't even have a spoon to my name. We didn't have much to begin with, we were living in a tiny three-room apartment, and we had no insurance, so in some ways that meant we lost even more than if we had owned a home at the time. But I was less upset that all of my stuff was gone, and mostly overwhelmed as we faced rebuilding with thoughts of, "Where in the world do we *start*?" when we had nothing except the donated clothes on our backs.

For some there is a deep need to explain why something like this happens. For me, it was simply cause and effect: Driver ran a light, missed a curb, and caused massive destruction in our tiny town, leaving the residents of three apartments homeless, two businesses destroyed, and an entire community in mourning but also grateful that it wasn't worse. I don't need any more explanation than that. I don't believe everything happens for a reason, unless that reason is simply faulty brakes. But I do need to find meaning in the aftermath of all things, not the least of all *big* things. And that's where writing comes in for me. In the words, I seek my truth.

Yet sometimes it's still a question of, "Where do I start?" Sometimes I stare at a blank page just like we once looked at empty rooms that we had to figure out how to refurnish in a matter of days versus the lifetimes in which we had acquired our belongings the first time around. It gradually came together between donations and new purchases and slowly our life began to look similar to what it had been, with some tweaks. Writing is similar. If you simply start putting words down, there's always something to come back to and polish. Something to think about deeper upon each round of revising. Something to fall back on when you're feeling lost. Words become a scaffolding that transcends emptiness. With everything I write I hope readers (including myself) will take away the combination of accepting uncertainty *and* always asking more questions. Because I truly believe that is what makes us a resilient, creative people. And that's what moves us forward with or without answers.

Science. Mystery. Art. Albert Einstein said, "The most beautiful experience we can have is the mysterious. It is the fundamental emotion that stands at the cradle of true art and true science." I am not a religious person but I think the three pillars of mystery, art, and science come together in a "triumvirate" of humanity. And those ideas contain enough spirituality to keep me seeking and writing and making meaning out of this life forever, through all the questions. I don't know why bad things happen. But I don't know why good things happen either. Sometimes there is no why. And yet, I will watch, and appreciate with wonder, a bumblebee gathering nectar on his impossibly-sized body. I'll listen to the treefrogs chirp a symphony of love and marvel at how a firefly will always make his way to the tippity-top of my fingertip before taking flight. I will always write, and lift my face to the stars and dream.

JESS RINKER is an award-winning writer who has several books for young readers including picture book biographies, chapter books, and middle grade fiction. In addition to writing for children, Jess's creative nonfiction has been featured in Feminine Collective, Creative Parents, Family Circle Magazine, PA Theatre Guide, Hunger Mountain, and other publications.

She and her husband, Joe McGee, also a children's author, have a little haven on the side of a mountain in West Virginia where they can write and enjoy everything the great outdoors has to offer. Except mosquitos. They can bug off.

Responding to the Unknown: Creativity as Both Answer and Inspiration

LIZ GARTON SCANLON

For years now there's been more unknown than known, more new than old, and more change than constant—for all of us. We're turned upside down daily, thanks to political and social and climatic shocks and upheaval.

As adults, as parents and educators and creators, we're asked to respond to all of it with grace and wisdom and nearly impossible foresight, with calm and undeterred conviction, in a way that comforts kids but also models for them how to navigate it all. But first, before we can model anything, we have to take in and make sense of the nonsensical ourselves, and for many of us that happens on the page.

I started writing for children the year my eldest was born and she's 26 now. Artists talk a lot about whether it's possible to immerse yourself in your own artistic endeavors and be a parent at the same time. Whether they will have the time and headspace necessary to be artistically brilliant—or even artistically mediocre—while changing diapers or packing lunches. But in my case, art and parenting are inextricable. My daughters delivered me right back into the world of children's books that I had loved when I was a kid. And, in keeping with the theme of this essay, they did so via the sweeping and massive change that babies and children impose on one's life.

I've published many books since those early days, books that vary widely in content and theme and aesthetic. But as a whole, they mark a more than 25-year period of my life that I wrote through. I wrote through having and raising children, losing a house to a flood, the realities of 9-11, my husband's cancer, the death of all four of my grandparents, numerous presidencies, the invention of flash drives, Facebook and cauliflower crust pizza, several of the best dogs and cats in the world, my daughters' stitches, seizures and college application seasons, an insurrection, a global pandemic, and empty nesting.

It was a lot. Too much, maybe. But I wrote through all of it, the same way some of you did. The way some of you drew and some of you cooked and some of you sang like angels.

Mary Shelley said, "Nothing is so painful to the human mind as a great and sudden change." Mélanie Watt (via her character *Scaredy Squirrel*) concurred: "The unknown can be a scary place for a squirrel." And it's true—the shifting sands of reality and the inscrutable map through the dunes can be both scary and painful.

Luckily, we humans were born with a powerful antidote—a powerful response system to change—built into our heads, our hearts, and our DNA. Creativity is our birthright. Creativity is where we go and what we do when faced with change, with struggle, trouble, surprise, and stress.

A recent study showed that art-making of any kind, from doodling to painting pottery to tying the knots of macrame, has positive health benefits, including a dramatic reduction in the stress hormone cortisol. This is something many of us, the lucky ones, have experienced and understand on some kind of intuitive level. We know creativity as an act, a process. A comfort, a way to heal, to ground and to settle. Knitting, journaling, painting, cooking, playing the piano—these are human balms, release valves, and meditations. They provide an actual physical answer to the chaos and noise and mysteries of life.

This is true for folks who identify as artists and those who don't, for those who are grown up, and those who aren't. As David Bayles and Ted Orland say in their book *Art & Fear*: "Art is made by ordinary people. Creatures having only virtues can hardly be imagined making art. It's difficult to picture the Virgin Mary painting landscapes. Or Batman throwing pots. The flawless creature wouldn't need to make art." As not-at-all flawless people, the act of creating, of engaging creatively with our lives on this planet, is quite simply how we find our way through them.

What I'm talking about here, of course, is the act

of doing and of making, the *verb*, the cortisol-releasing process of creating. But there is also the noun. That which is made. The product, the gift. Forever, we humans have listened to music and lost ourselves in museums, and read book after book after book seeking a way to understand what is happening and why, seeking a way to calm and comfort ourselves, seeking companions in the abyss and on the journey.

There is a deeply human, deeply grounding, deeply comforting reason there are so many books about grief, about navigating new schools, about garden variety fears of all kinds (none of which really turn out to be garden variety!). We don't even need modern, pedagogical phrasing like "social emotional learning" to understand why these books are what we need and where we go when everything changes, when the ground gets wobbly, when so little feels right, or safe, or known.

There is a reason we read aloud to brand new babies, to story-time circles, and to kids of all ages, ready for bed—and it's not just for the kids. Because, like the doodlers and cooks and knitters whose cortisol levels are lowered by *being* creative, those of us who absorb and take in and engage with art feel better, too.

So, yes, at every level, creativity is an answer—a comforting, safe, reflective, empathic response to change and surprise and struggle. But what if change and surprise and struggle can also, counterintuitively, symbiotically, serve as inspiration for our creative practices?

I want to suggest that creativity isn't just there to catch us after a fall, to answer our questions and our wailing cries. That it doesn't just respond to change but springs from it. Creativity and new ideas and brave steps forward—these things turn big changes and dark days into opportunities for growth—not just for us, but for our characters and our young readers.

Kelly Barnhill in *When Women Were Dragons* doesn't disagree with Mary Shelley in *Frankenstein* or Mélanie Watt in *Scaredy Squirrel*: the changes Barnhill depicts in her novel—women turning to dragons!—are dramatic and sudden and, yes, painful. But, she says (or rather, her character Alex says), "Everything changes. Everything starts out as one thing and then turns into another. It's part of being alive."

"Am I a seed?" her cousin Beatrice asks her a little later. "Maybe," answers Alex.

We *are* seeds, all of us. We possess an incredible capacity for bursting open, for growing up, for bearing creative fruit in the face of challenge and discord. Indeed, it's worth saying something wildly obvious here, and that is that growing up *is all about* change. This idea of change and growth being braided together is baked in, is who we've always been.

I'll return to the book *Art & Fear* here. "Uncertainty," Orland and Bayles say, "is the essential, inevitable and all-pervasive companion to your desire to make art." In other words, change is our creative engine.

It's true, isn't it, that many of our books come from places of confusion and disempowerment and lack of agency? Baffling times are the source of story. And this gets even more meta (and more interesting) when our characters themselves face and respond to change with, inevitability, creativity!

In my picture book *Another Way to Climb a Tree*, a child too sick to play outdoors uses her fingers to climb the shadow a tree has cast on her wall. In *Kate, Who Tamed the Wind*, our hero helps manage the battering effects of climate change by delivering a wagonload of saplings to an old man living at the tip-top of a steep, windswept hill and, together, they plant them. And in *One Dark Bird*, the characters aren't even people—they're birds—but still they know how to react when faced with sudden, terrifying change. The birds had been flying alone until danger arrives in the form of a predator and they "become a flock," forming a murmuration—one of the more naturally creative responses to fear that there is.

It's simple. All of these characters answer the disruption in their lives with creative acts. And yes, picture books offer up especially good, concise examples but this idea, that authors—and our characters—are inspired by—and respond creatively to—tumult and loss and mystery and change, holds true for other forms, too.

Remember Kelly Barnhill's *When Women Were Dragons* where the characters, literally respond to the challenges—and the emptiness—in their lives by transforming into dragons?

So back to our birthright for a moment, our intuitive human response to the mysteries and chasms and losses and seismic shifts life offers up again and again and again. Creativity is what so often comforts and grounds and heals and supports us—both the doing and, also, the consuming. But what a joy to realize that the inevitable mysteries and chasms and losses and seismic shifts also inspire creative acts and can result in rather ingenious realization, movement, and growth.

I want to wrap this up by coming back to young readers specifically. Young humans. When they see us adults responding creatively to the things we're afraid of, to the things we don't like or understand, when they see our *characters* responding creatively, when they see our characters actually being *inspired* by fear, or emptiness or great change—they begin to feel capable of responding creatively themselves.

They are, indeed, seeds. We are all seeds, and our world is a messy, crowded, undone plot. But we know, deep in our bones, how to dig in and do what's necessary. How to turn over the soil. How to respond to fear and loss with creative acts of our own, as parents and educators and artists. So our characters and our young readers can do the same when they need to.

LIZ GARTON SCANLON is the award-winning, New York Times bestselling author of more than 25 picture books, chapter books, and middle grade novels. She's served on faculty for the Vermont College of Fine Arts and Whale Rock Workshops, and she lives and writes in Austin, Texas.

Living is Creating, Creating is Resiliency

EMMA SHALAWAY

I've struggled with accepting myself as a *writer* for most of my life. While I have always written—whether it be short stories, screenplays, or journal entries—I've never fully recognized this to be a part of my true identity. Even when I moved to Los Angeles, working full time in the film industry, I felt like I was not "creative enough" to view myself as an artist.

Although I've noticed that writing has always been something I have leaned on heavily when processing grief. From helplessly watching my city burn, to seeing my family's community swept away by floods, to navigating the loss of my father, I've always turned to writing as a way through hard times.

Journaling is an outlet to clear my brain—get all the racing thoughts out. Feelings I'm too embarrassed to share can be released onto a page in a notebook—

or more often the Notes app on my phone—that no one ever has to read. Frustrations can be written down and acknowledged so I can let them go. Ideas can be explored to enable more nuanced conversations around these emotionally-charged topics.

Additionally, I find myself looking for answers in the writing of others. In times of anguish, I can bury myself in the words of a stranger to help navigate the way forward. Whether the writer is an expert on the climate crisis, an award-winning novelist, or simply another human sharing their thoughts from their own unique lived experience, the words of others can temporarily become the vocabulary for my brain to process the challenging situations that every human on this earth encounters at some point. They provide a script to mimic in times when darkness obscures my ability to put my own feelings into words, affording me the opportunity to connect and foster community amidst the pain and temporary loss of words.

I finally had an epiphany. Emotions are a human superpower. They can save us and they can destroy us, if we let them. When they're positive, we believe anything is possible and appear to glide through life, in perfect alignment with the universe. When we are struck with negative emotions it can feel as if we are living in a Munch painting, with accentuating dark thoughts shrouding our entire outlook and existence. If left unchecked, these emotional tides can overtake our perception of reality, shielding us from the infinite possibilities and synchronicities this world offers daily. The creative process is a conduit for these feelings to flow through us—not getting stuck within, weighing us down.

Writing is a catalyst for the evolution of thought—within ourselves and within our communities. While journaling, I uncover insights that concretize on the page and sporadically find their way into conversations. To my surprise (and delight) several people have stopped me mid-conversation to reflect on what I had shared. In that moment, it opened their mind to a new way of seeing a situation or provided comfort previously inaccessible to them. I realized creativity is not something people do, it is a fundamental part of who we are. Writing builds connection and strengthens empathy. It awakens us to the shared experience of the human condition. Reminding us that despite differing catalysts for our feelings, we likely have more overlap in our internal struggles than we think.

The creative process is a cycle that begins with the emotions of being utterly human. It continues as we transmute those feelings into a creative outlet—words, pictures, music, dance. Now these feelings are out of our bodies and in the world. We can decide if we want to share them with others or maybe the process of getting them out of our head was all that was needed. If we choose to share our creations, a larger cycle continues, encouraging others to reflect and build upon our own thoughts. This cycle provides value to both groups—the creator gets an outlet and processing tool and the audience receives an outside perspective to aid in their own understanding and perseverance. The creative process is symbiotic for the creator and the audience, allowing for a progression of thought and evolved empathy for the human experience that is shared by all, giving way to personal and communal resiliency.

Ultimately, our identity as *writer* or *artist* is irrelevant. What matters is that we are creating and contributing to our community. Whether we are looking to process the emotions that accompany the loss of a loved one, explore complicated feelings that arise in personal relationships, or are looking for hope while observing the growing devastation of natural disasters, the creative cycle aids us in accepting whatever we are feeling. It shows us how these feelings strengthen our connection to one another and allows us to move forward on a more resilient path.

EMMA SHALAWAY is a national marketing director, environmental activist, and queer neurodivergent creative. When she's not at her desk, she's most likely surfing, hiking with her cattle dog Loki, yoga-ing, or pulling Tarot cards. She currently lives in Long Beach, CA. Connect with her on Instagram @eshalaway.

At the Edge of the Dark, Dark Wood

MEGAN SHEPHERD

It was summer when we took over the farm. I had no gardening experience. I told my husband I wasn't worried because I liked that romantic "wild garden" look—overgrown beds straight out of *The Secret Garden*, with vines growing up the fences at the edge of the property where it was half-wild anyway. I got my wish, and in classic fairy tale fashion, it might have been more of a curse. Within days the garden was less charmingly wild and more of a green inferno. I imagined that long ago, the original farmer on our land had traded his soul in return for such rich soil, until I realized that the soil didn't need magic to be productive—it had a hundred years' worth of dairy cows' natural fertilizer.

I adopted the old farm office as my writing cottage, dragging in second-hand furniture and bookshelves, fighting the bees living in the walls, the birds nesting in the rafters, the groundhog in the foundation. It was frigid in winter and sweltering in summer, but I kept returning to it. Even in January it smelled like wood pitch, a smell that took me back to my summers at camp, and gave me that endless summertime feeling, when magic and lightning bugs were in the air, and responsibilities wouldn't start again until August. There, I was free to dream. Deadlines and emails were distant—those belonged across the yard and up the stairs in my formal office in our farmhouse, where I handled business.

Like most writers, I live with my head in the clouds—so I keep my feet in the soil. To feel rooted in the real world, connected to the creatures and people who walked here before us, who made a living from the earth. People don't change much. We retell fairy tales written hundreds of years ago because people are still just as jealous and foolish and hopeful as those princes and princesses long ago. "Beware of strangers bearing gifts," the myth of ancient Troy tells us, and *yeah*. Thousands of years later, we are all still just wide-eyed neophytes discovering the same old advice, over and over.

The Holy Grail that every writer seeks is balance, and here's a secret: we'll never get it. To be a writer you have to be tilted dangerously toward obsession. Most writers I know can be described as ambitious, unpredictable, teetering between overconfidence and a devastating lack thereof. It's only in nature that I can step outside of my ambition and remember that the ants parading up the blueberry bushes don't give a shit about my stories—there's something comforting in that. In nature, on the farm, life moves forward with the steady predetermination of the seasons and nothing can interfere with that, not even editors. If it wasn't for the seasons, I'm not sure I'd ever look up from my desk. But when snow buries the chicken coop, I have no choice but to pay attention to worlds outside of the ones I'm creating on a page. To put on pants—the bane of every stay-at-home writer—and exercise more than my creativity. And it's usually in these moments, digging a path for my chickens in the snow, that I can finally breathe. I won't say that my best ideas come to me while gardening, because they don't—I'm too busy cussing out some crappy root that has gotten in the way of my shovel. But it stretches my mind to allow space for those stories to come later, to fill in the gaps.

I'm fighting my inclination to make a tidy list of all the ways writing books is like gardening: pruning out words, sowing the seeds of ideas, and so on. Anything can be analogous to writing if you try hard enough—and a lot of writers have, myself included. But I know this is true: whenever I am asked my best advice for teenage writers, I tell them: read widely (or risk a watered-down, overly familiar voice), write often (because butt-in-chair), and live boldly. It's that last one where their eyes glaze over. Mine would have done the same at their age. Because *that is so not helpful*. I tell them that they need to write from life experience. They don't need to know what it's like to survive on Mars or fight dinosaurs, but they do need to know what real fear, love, and desire feel like. Too often, I forget to take my own advice, and somehow days pass and I begin to resemble Johnny Depp's slovenly paranoid writer in *Secret Window*. But then the farm calls. The chickens won't wait—or rather, the foxes, at dusk, licking their chops, won't.

On the farm I grow lavender and basil and rosemary, and hang it to dry in our farmhouse, and make it into tea that grows cold and forgotten in a mug on my desk, while I'm writing about witches who grow lavender and basil and rosemary for love potions. Once, a lost elk wandered onto our land and took a dip in our pond, never mind that the closest elk herd is 50 miles away. I put on pants and went outside for that one. One night I woke up to the reek of billowing smoke. Convinced the house was on fire, I shook my husband awake and grabbed my dog—only to realize there was no smoke. It hadn't been a dream, I was sure. A hallucination? A vision? When I mentioned it to the neighbors who have lived in our valley for decades, they warned me about the history of fires on our farm. In the 1950s, a caretaker couple on the property died in bed when their cottage caught fire. In 2005, a New Year's Eve party ended in tragedy when a candle lit the drapes on fire, badly burning the previous owner. In 2011, the historic 30-stall dairy barn, lovingly converted into a library of rare books, burned down in such an inferno that everyone in town remembers it. When we bought the farmhouse, the previous owners warned us that it was cursed. They'd even gone so far as to remove all the fireplaces, including the ones dating back to the 1800s. I didn't tell them that the first thing my husband and I did, when renovating, was install a wood stove smack in the middle of the house. Since then I've woken up nights with more hallucinations—my vision turns red as though the house is engulfed in flames. The doorbell rings in the middle of the night and no one is there. Is my farmstead part of a fairytale or a ghost story?

In spring, after the snowmelt, my dog uncovers artifacts in the creek bed—old bottles, a tin milk jug from its dairy farm days, the bones of small animals, shed snakeskins left on our porch, old crystal doorknobs. We keep these objects in a curio cabinet and, when I'm in need of inspiration, I rifle through the birds' nests and mice skulls, making up macabre little stories in my mind. In winter, I'll track the deer prints in the snow to the gully to see where they make their home. I like to think that wolves are watching from a distance, ready to snatch my picnic basket—though wolves have long been gone from the bordering forests. Then again, so have elk. Just as rare is a story that catches fire, and I think that's really what I'm looking for, spending so many sweltering hours with my hands in the dirt. Life on a farm is synonymous with constant change, but stories might live forever, or as long as the internet and the Library of Congress persist. And immortality is a wish even the Brothers Grimm might find suitably ambitious.

MEGAN SHEPHERD is the New York Times bestseller and Carnegie Medal-nominated author of many acclaimed novels for readers of all ages. She lives and writes on a haunted 130-year-old farm outside Asheville, North Carolina, with her husband and children, cats, chickens, bees, and an especially scruffy dog.

What We Carry in Our Guts

LINDSEY STODDARD

When I was twelve, my dad got a new job and we moved an hour a half away from my old school, my classmates and friends, my soccer and swim teams. I was mad and lonely and nervous that I wouldn't find my place. My old house had a neighborhood with cul-de-sacs and kids who would run with me through our connected backyards and into the woods until our parents called us home for dinner with the blasts of air horns. My new house was out a rolling dirt road, up a long driveway, surrounded by acres of trees, and felt very, very far away. The only thing that excited me, at first, about our new house was a perfectly flat stretch of land right at the bottom of our new yard's hill where my parents said we could try to dig a pond. I imagined a little dock and cattails and catching frogs.

In order for there to be a pond, there had to be water,

so my dad called my grandpa. He came the next day and brought with him a big stick shaped like a capital Y.

"My dowsing stick," Grandpa said, when I asked him what it was. He let me run my fingers along the smoothed apple tree branch. "It'll tell me what we need to know, if there's water down there or not," he said with his old voice that sounded full of gravel and wood chips and maple sap that had been hardened to the bark.

He headed down to the clearing, and held each fork of the Y in his upturned fists as he walked across the land, step by slow step, waiting for the branch to turn and point down toward any water there might be collecting beneath the earth.

I sat at the top of the hill, watching him step, slowly, then stop, and step again, and I remember thinking that my grandpa was made of magic. That the sawdust that clung to all his flannel shirts and stuck to the leather of his work boots must actually be fairy dust, star dust. That he had some special connection with the land that he could feel up through the bottoms of his boots, and deep inside him all the way to his fingertips. That he didn't simply spend his days walking through nature, he had sprouted up from it. That he was made of rushing water, and opening buds, of running sap, and wind-blown dandelion seeds. He was made of earth.

My grandpa was losing his memory during those days, sometimes forgetting where he was, and the ends of his sentences, and sometimes forgetting the names for things. "Your granddaughter," I'd remind him. "Lindsey." He'd nod ever so slightly like that wasn't the important thing, because he knew how to find what was underneath.

He spent less and less time talking as I was growing up, but in that moment, watching him step and stop, step and stop, I knew, for certain, that he hadn't forgotten how to listen. That some things we just carry in our guts, and it doesn't require us to remember because they'll always be there.

This memory of my grandpa, searching for water with his dowsing stick in our new yard is at the core of my most recent middle grade novel, *The Real Deal*. In that book, I wanted to explore all the things we carry in our guts, the things we know to be right and the things that feel wrong, memories that we could never lose, the things that scare us, the things we can't possibly fix, and the things that bring us hope.

While writing this book, another one of those gut-memories came to live on the surface for me. The winter after we moved, just months after my grandpa searched for water beneath the earth, a friend and classmate from my old school died from an unlucky, unfair, and horrific accident in the classroom. I started lodging the grief and guilt beneath, in my guts. If I had been there, I thought, if we hadn't moved, maybe I would have called my friend over in that awful moment, out of danger, to look at something in my backpack, or to help me with a stuck zipper, or to sneak a game of tic-tac-toe in my notebook. My twelve-year-old mind played out all the possible scenes, the *what-ifs* and the *maybes*, and I carried them with me. Maybe my presence would have shifted the universe enough to make it a close, scary call instead of what it was. Or maybe, it would have fallen on me.

The whole community—my friends and classmates from my old town who showed up at school and faced her empty seat, the teachers, and administrators, and all the grown-ups charged with caring for children—grieved, and felt loss, and acted out the pain in their guts in different ways. And I stuffed mine down inside with the distance, and the helplessness, and the new understanding that unspeakably terrible things can happen to really good people.

I began writing *The Real Deal* during a very hard year for our country, for our world. We were sheltering-in from a global pandemic. We were scared, and uncertain, and grieving the loss of so many lives and jobs and connections. We were angry and broken over the murder of George Floyd, and searching for hope.

At times, this book felt impossible to write. And one time, before I ever really began, I quit. I told my husband that I was giving up for now, that it was too much to manage while caring for our young children and trying to filter for them the weight of the world. I closed my notebooks and put down my pen, but he listened and listened as I spilled my guts about distance and loneliness and loss and the connections that made me feel stronger and more hopeful, and he very quietly, and very lovingly, wouldn't let me give up.

So, with the memory of my grandpa silently walking the land, listening, and searching for water beneath the surface, and with the memory of my old classmate and friend, and the understanding that we all carry things in our guts, and with my children and for my children, and for twelve-year-old Lindsey and all her old schoolmates and friends and teachers, and with the consistent support of family, I wrote. I wrote about Gabe and Oliver, and their deep and loving friendship. I wrote about their delight for graphic novels, and the comic they're creating together in school. And I wrote about the new kid, Reuben, who doesn't talk, not ever. I wrote their gut-secrets, and I wrote their laughter.

The Real Deal became a story about grief and coping and hope. It's a story about connections, the ones we refuse to give up, and the new ones we are brave enough to create. It's an ode to the things that bring us joy: Books we freely choose to read, Vermont maple creemees, drawing, and art, and teachers who celebrate stories and inspire creativity, exploring the woods, and riding your bicycle through town, and true, deep friendships with holds beneath the surface. It's a standing up to the things we refuse to accept, a story about recognizing the way things are, and creating a path to something better. It's about holding onto your people, listening to your guts, and becoming the realest deal version of your own self.

All of this is the work of writers, particularly those who write for children. We hold out our hands, and with slow steps, we walk the land of our memories. We walk, and listen, and we wait for the ones that pull at us strongly, showing that there is something down there worth digging for.

We remember the small moments that made us feel big things: a forgotten name, our grandpa's steps. And we remember the big moments that made us feel small: a move to a new town, an accident that shook a community to its core. And we write our hearts out, through the hurt in our guts and the hurt of the world, shining light on the joys we could never forget, so that children everywhere will feel less alone.

LINDSEY STODDARD is the critically-acclaimed author of five middle grade novels including <u>Just Like Jackie</u>, <u>Brave Like That</u>, and <u>The Real Deal</u>. She was born and raised in Vermont, where she grew up hiking along the Appalachian Trail, playing in the snow, and eating Ben & Jerry's ice cream. She spent twelve years living in NYC and teaching middle school English in an amazing little school called MS 324 in the neighborhood of Washington Heights. Lindsey received her MFA in Creative Writing for Children and Young Adults from Vermont College of Fine Arts, and now resides back in Vermont with her husband, two children, and their dog.

Becoming a Writer

MEERA TREHAN

It was the last day of my first writing class as an adult, and I was happily feeding my meter with quarters I'd fished out of my cupholder. The previous week had been a good one, writing-wise: I'd submitted my first story for the class—a picture book that had lived in my head for years, and I'd finally gotten down on paper. And based on a talk my instructor had given on character development and tension, I'd come up with an idea for a novel about an Indian-American family that moves from the Bay Area to a small town in Virginia on the eve of 9/11. As my last coin disappeared into the meter, I noticed my instructor parked just a few spaces away. We began chatting in the lot about this and that when I decided to tell her.

"So," I said. "I have this idea…"

I didn't grow up wanting to be a writer. As a kid,

I didn't dream of filling notebooks in practiced cursive or, when the technology changed, pecking out pages of brilliant prose on my laptop. Though I was a voracious reader, I didn't identify with the actual human beings who wrote the books I loved. Perhaps more to the point, it didn't occur to me I could be one of them. I'd written poems, but entire books? Those were beyond me. Even as I got older and I began to think of authors with a mix of awe and envy, I was pretty sure I lacked whatever magic let them write a book from start to finish. Besides, I wanted to be a lawyer. So I went to law school, became a lawyer, and am glad I did.

But life isn't always predictable, and after over a decade of practicing law I found myself in that classroom on a July day awaiting feedback on my picture book draft. We'd done craft exercises every session—which I found both fun and instructive—but this was the first time I'd submitted work ahead of time. As the instructor said my name, there was a split-second pause when, at least for me, the mood shifted. I knew in that moment I would not be receiving the feedback I hoped for—which was, of course, "It's absolutely perfect." I would not even be getting, "It's absolutely perfect, except for this *one* thing."

Unfortunately, like many adults writing their first picture book, I'd seriously underestimated the difficulty of the task. My draft was long on words and short on voice and nowhere close to any definition of perfect. Nevertheless, my instructor's feedback, though not sugar-coated, was respectful and took my work seriously. She discussed the characters and reviewed the craft elements, while I took notes, glumly, because I knew I'd missed the mark. My first attempt at a story was not what I'd hoped. But then, out of nowhere, she said with a burst of genuine enthusiasm, "What you really should be writing is that novel about the sisters."

What?

The story I'd mentioned in the parking lot?

In theory, this was not bad advice. But as a practical matter, it was impossible. I wasn't a writer, and I certainly wasn't a novelist. It wasn't that I didn't *want* to write that book. It's just that I couldn't. I couldn't sustain an idea for the entire course of a novel. I couldn't build a set of scenes into a chapter or a set of chapters into a book. I didn't understand story structure. I didn't get how to integrate theme. Frankly, as a writing teacher and professional author, my instructor should have understood that better than me.

I had, however, really enjoyed the class. So even though I couldn't write a novel, I decided I could go out and get one of the books she'd recommended and work through the craft exercises. I couldn't write a novel, but I could check out stacks of picture books from the library and analyze the interplay between text and art. I couldn't write a novel, but I could—with starts and stops—study writing through mentor texts, conference talks, more classes, and other writers.

My not-writing-a-novel phase lasted for years. But though I wasn't writing that story I'd told my instructor about, it still stayed with me. A town grew around my fictional family, and they began to interact with long-time friends and questionable neighbors. They became less characters that I'd imagined in response to an exercise, and more people trying to tell me about their journey, if I could only get it down. At times, I tried, but never made it past the first few pages. I still wasn't sure where to begin. Nevertheless, I was learning—not just about writing, but also about identifying the tools I needed to get better.

Eventually, what I needed most of all was to learn how to get more words on the page. So, I enrolled in an aptly named workshop, "How to Write a Lot." In that workshop, the teacher discussed a number of strategies that I found helpful and incorporated into my writing practice. But she also made a larger point: If this is something you want to do, you owe it to yourself to try.

Soon after, I began working on that novel I'd first talked about in the parking lot. I wrote a highly imperfect story (it lacked an ending, for starters), but it was, at least in the loosest sense of the word, a draft. After a break, I tried to focus on the one or two things I wanted to work on in the next draft. When I finished my second draft, I did the same for my third, and then my fourth, until eventually I had a novel-shaped story that I believed in.

It is at this point in the essay that I would like to say this novel was published beautifully, and you can find it at booksellers everywhere. I would like to, but I can't. After months of querying, I received offers of representation and signed with an agent. The book, however, did not sell.

I'm not going to lie—it was tough getting that close to publication and falling short. But as always, there were lessons to be learned (though not on embracing rejection—please!). I learned to work on my next novel while waiting for news on the first. I learned how important it is to me to be a part of a community of writers who understand the ups and downs of publishing. And perhaps most importantly, I learned what my instructor had been trying to tell me all along: By doing the work, you already are a writer.

Meera Trehan
Chevy Chase, MD
2024

MEERA TREHAN is the author of two critically acclaimed middle grade novels, THE VIEW FROM THE VERY BEST HOUSE IN TOWN *and* SNOW, *both of which are published in multiple countries. She practiced public interest law for over a decade before turning to creative writing. She lives in Maryland with her family. Find her online at meeratrehan.com*

Body Language: Acting Out, Scenes Without Obscene Gestures, and Other Effective Ways to Show Emotion

PADMA VENKATRAMAN

Dialogue is immensely important, but not every character is chatty. Even chatterboxes sometimes express themselves through actions, rather than through words. Before we learn how to speak, we understand and express ourselves through nonverbal cues. Yet, as writers, we tend to focus on dialogue (after all, words are our trade).

Body language is, however, an important way in which characters characterize themselves. Interspersing body language carefully between snippets of dialogue can show the reader a great deal: it can convey emotion, deepen character, provide an insight into the current status of relationships among characters, and allow us to see how a character feels about a particular setting.

When a character is lying, nonverbal clues become especially important and body language can give away the truth. For example, a character's facial expression when he's apologizing to the school principal may reveal whether he's truly sorry or pretending to apologize.

Body language isn't restricted to facial expression. If your heroine usually stands erect, seeing her slump in one scene will immediately communicate to your reader that something is amiss. Body language includes a person's posture, stance, gait, hand gestures, mannerisms and visceral reactions that we can't control (such as butterflies in the stomach).

Speaking of butterflies, avoid clichés when you incorporate body language into your writing. Personalize and particularize a character's body language just as you would his speech. We tend to modify our body language depending on where we are and to whom we're reacting. If your hero suffers a loss, he may cry when he's alone, but act stoically in front of his friends.

Although there are many books devoted to writing good dialogue and few that deal with using nonverbal cues, there's no dearth of outside resources on body language.

Study serious graphic novels, but don't restrict yourself to them. Pore over comic strips in your favorite newspaper. Caricaturists often exaggerate facial expressions, but they also capture the truth. Watch animated films. Visit art museums and see how the artists portray emotion and character. Draw stick figures showing how your characters are positioned during important scenes.

As a writer, you're probably used to eavesdropping on other people's conversations. Try adamsdropping—okay, so that's my new word—watch people who're too far away to hear, and try to figure out what they're saying and how they're feeling, based on their body language.

Study your favorite actor or actress. How does he/she use the body to communicate? Watch a foreign language film (without subtitles) in a language you don't know. Can you understand the emotional backdrop? Do you get a sense of character? How do nonverbal cues in this culture differ from your own?

Diversity adds an important dimension to nonverbal cues. Clicking the tongue signals irritation and disapproval in some cultures, but is a sign of sympathy in others.

Don't overlook the power of acting and trying to get into character. When I was writing *A Time to Dance*, I immersed myself in the life of my character by walking on crutches up and down stairs, doing unusual things like tying up my leg when I went to bed, and experimenting on myself to simulate phantom pain. My attempt to "go method" (the way an actress might) paid off when a reader, who had had an amputation, was shocked to discover I hadn't had one and exclaimed, "But you know exactly what phantom pain feels like!"

Once you begin to study body language, you'll find yourself learning everywhere you go.

PADMA VENKATRAMAN *is the author of* The Bridge Home, Born Behind Bars, A Time to Dance, Island's End, *and* Climbing the Stairs. *Her books have sold over ¼ million copies, received over 20 starred reviews, and won numerous awards: Walter Dean Myers Award, South Asia Book Award, Golden Kite, ALA Notable, etc. Her poetry has been published in Poetry Magazine and nominated for a Pushcart Prize. Safe Harbor, her latest novel (for children in grades 3-6), is inspired by her experience as a BIPOC female oceanographer. When she's not writing, Padma loves teaching and sharing her love for reading and writing with others. Visit her at www.padmavenkatraman.com or arrange a visit via The Author Village.*

Inside Out: Creating Voice Through Building Your Character

ALEXANDRA VILLASANTE

Voice is the difference between prose that lies flat and plays dead, and words that skip, race, bolt for the hills. Voice will keep a reader holding on through the difficult scenes, the uncomfortable chapters, the unlikable characters.

Voice can make the reader fall in love.

Okay, fine, good. But what IS voice, and more importantly, how do we create it?

Voice encompasses the unique style, tone, and perspective through which a story is told.

It exists in relation to an author, book, and characters (yes, *all* the characters, even the secondary and background characters!). By drilling down on specific word choices, you create a unique feeling or viewpoint—in fact, you create your characters.

Because, voice reveals personality, attitudes and

emotions. It affects, even subconsciously, how readers perceive and engage with your story by evoking emotional or intellectual responses and contributing to the overall theme of a story.

Not for nothing, but voice is a *big* deal.

If we look in our writer's toolbox (or cookbook, or witch's almanac—take your pick of metaphor), the recipe for voice seems deceptively simple:

Voice = Word Choice + Rhythm

(I cribbed that from Linda Sue Park; writers are all magpies, borrowing from each other—and giving credit where credit is due.)

- Word choice is vocabulary—including languages, cultural references, slang, repetition, verbal tics.
- Rhythm is sentence length, paragraph length, punctuation, cadence.

That's it. But it's not the whole story.

There are three kinds of voice in writing:

Authorial Voice - The vocabulary, cultural, and societal references, stylistic choices the author favors across different works

Narrative/Book Voice - The vocabulary, stylistic choices, world-building specific environment of the book (regardless of POV)

Character Voice - The vocabulary, stylistic choices, emotional state, sensory state, view of self and others, memory

Here are some examples of the different kinds of voice.

AUTHORIAL VOICE: JANE AUSTEN

"It is a truth universally acknowledged, that a single man in possession of a good fortune, must be in want of a wife."
- *Pride & Prejudice*

"The family of Dashwood had been long settled in Sussex. Their estate was large, and their residence was at Norland Park, in the centre of their property, where for many generations, they had lived in so respectable a manner as to engage the general good opinion of their surrounding acquaintance."
- *Sense & Sensibility*

"Emma Woodhouse, handsome, clever, and rich, with a comfortable home and happy disposition, seemed to unite some of the best blessings of existence; and had lived nearly twenty one years in the world with very little to distress or vex her."
- *Emma*

NARRATIVE/BOOK VOICE

First person
"'Wolfman's got nards!' That was the best line of any movie ever!" Sam shouted in the empty theater. There had been a couple in the back, but they'd left before the movie ended. More people should have appreciated The Monster Squad when it was in theaters. I guess they had cooler stuff to do, like drive their girlfriends to the mall. Tiffany's boyfriend, Brooks, was so lucky. He dressed like a preppie fool, but maybe that was what she liked. That and his car.
- *Dead Flip* by Sara Farizan

Second person
Today you are a beggar, your preferred disguise during the wintertime. You are curled into a ball but still stretch across two seats at the far end of the subway car. Your hands are buried in your pockets, and you caress the tattered photo hidden in its depths. You are alone—but not for long.
- *Beware the Empty Subway Car* by Maika Moulite and Maritza Moulite (*Our Shadows Have Claws: 15 Latin American Monster Stories*)

Third person
"The Moose is a lie," Stevie Bell said. Her mother turned to her, looking like she often looked—a bit tired, forced to engage in whatever Stevie was about to say out of parental obligation.

"What?" she said.
Stevie pointed out the window of the coach.
"See that?" Stevie indicated a sign that simply read MOOSE. "We've passed five of those. That's a lot of promises. Not one moose"
- *Truly Devious* by Maureen Johnson

CHARACTER VOICE

Second Chances
Why is it that principals
Love giving second chances?
Love reminding me they were kids, too?
Love acting like they're doing me a favor,
doing my mom a favor,
by sitting me down all serious
and asking what they can do?
Well, guess what.
This is Seventh grade now,
and I don't need anyone's help but my own.
I've moved on from everything
that happened
I've made lists and I've made goals,
and if I'm in the principal's office,
you can 100% bet
that it wasn't my fault.
- *Iveliz Explains It All* by Andrea Beatriz Arango

Understanding what voice is, and all the ways it appears on the page is only the first part of the process.

The second part is knowing how to create that voice so it's specific, singular, recognizable, and utterly engrossing.

One way to do that is by building your characters from the inside out.

HOW TO BUILD A CHARACTER

ASK Your character - Who, what, where, when, how *Are You?*
- Identity
- Time period
- Environment
- Mental and physical health
- Socio-economic/class

NOTICE How they speak about themselves
- Contemporaneous language choices
- Sensory details of environment
- Emotional regulation/lack of
- Access to advantages, knowledge, confidence

When building character through voice, word choice is king. I could have said, word choice is *important*, or *crucial*, or *vital*. But by choosing the word *king*, I'm letting you know a bit about myself (I like a slightly unusual word choice) and I'm using a short, punchy word for effect.

Matthias, one of the main characters in the ensemble heist story, *Six of Crows* by Leigh Bardugo, struggles with contradictory words that flood his mind during a highly emotional and violent interaction:

"Nina," he gritted out. She clawed at his hands. "Witch," he hissed leaning over her.

He saw her eyes widen, her face getting redder. "Beg me," he said. "Beg me for your life." He heard a click, and a gravelly voice said, "Hands off her, Helvar."

Someone behind him had pressed a gun to his neck. Matthias didn't spare him a glance. "Go ahead and shoot me," he said. He dug his fingertips deeper into Nina's neck—nothing would deprive him of this. Nothing.

Traitor, witch, abomination. All those words came to him but others crowded in, too: beautiful, charmed one, *Röed fetla,* he'd called her, little red bird, for the color of her Grisha Order.

The intense drama of the moment juxtaposed with Matthias' battling words gives us insight into just how conflicted and lethal this character is.

In *The Girls I've Been* by Tess Sharp, Nora is the daughter of a con woman, who has been used in many, many cons, as many, many different characters. One of the ways the author grounds the reader's experience of Nora—who we know has lied and pretended to be other people—is to have Nora explain the process of being forced to become another "girl."

Rebecca. Sweet. Silent. Smiling.

One of my clearest early memories is my mother standing me in front of the mirror and combing blonde hair off my shoulders as she said, "Rebecca, your name is Rebecca. Say it sweetie. Rebecca Waitfield." My name isn't Rebecca, if you were wondering. It's not really Nora either, but everyone in Claire Creek knows me as Nora. I thought it was a game, the Rebecca thing, but later, Mom slaps my arm when I answer to anything but Rebecca, and I learn, it isn't a game. I learn, it's my life.

Even when a character isn't telling us the truth, *they're telling us true things about themselves*. None of this is Nora's doing, none of this is fun. Her mother's con lifestyle has become her whole life and there's nothing Nora can do about it.

EXERCISES

Spending some time digging into your character's voice is a great way to jump-start your writing when stalled, or start off a new project. Even if you're revising, it's never too late to take a closer look at voice.

Exercise One: Inside/Outside

Draw an outline of a person—like the shape of a gingerbread man cookie. This is your character. Outside of your character, list:
- Where they are
- Environment—anything from the room they're standing in, to the country they live in, to the weather they experience

- How they dress/how they look
- How much or little they think about their clothes, hair, makeup, accessories
- What they choose: objects, scents, music
- Where they go/want to go

Inside of your character, list:
- Who they say they are
- Who others say they are
- Their biggest fear
- What they want
- What stands in their way

Use this word-sketch to remember the internal and external factors that make up your character and make word and rhythm choices accordingly. If your character is a highly organized person who is abnormally fixated on time, they might wear a state-of-the-art watch and enable messages and alerts. That fact could translate into using short sentences and awkward pauses because they don't have the time to fully express themselves.

Exercise Two: The Closet

Imagine your character waking up, washing up, and getting dressed. Pause right there. Before they get dressed, have them open their closet door and look inside.
- What's your character's favorite clothing items (why)?
- Where do they keep their secrets? Their

memories?
- Where do they keep things that no longer fit?
- What are they ashamed of/guilty pleasure?
- What's something they put on that feels like armor?

The way your character choses to present themselves to the world is a part of the character's voice. Even without a word of dialogue, what they wear (or don't wear) can speak volumes about who they are.

In the end, voice is made up of the thousands of word choices you make for your characters, your books, and how you like to tell a story. Voice is the music of words.

ALEXANDRA VILLASANTE'S Young Adult novel, The Grief Keeper, won the 2020 Lambda Literary Award for LGBTQ Children's Literature/Young Adult Fiction and was a Junior Library Guild Gold Selection. Her next Young Adult novel, Fireblooms, publishes from Penguin Random House/Nancy Paulsen Books in September 2025.

Alex is a contributor to several Young Adult short story anthologies and is a co-founder of the Latinx Kidlit Book Festival and the Latinx Storytellers Conference. When she's not writing, painting, or planning, Alex works for the Highlights Foundation. You can visit Alex at www.alexandravillasante.com

Sometimes, Ya Gotta Pivot

LINDA WASHINGTON

I have always thought of auditions in regard to music, television, movie, or theatrical productions like *A Chorus Line, Rent, Wicked,* etc. Since I never had aspirations for a career in the theater ("thea-TAH" is how I pronounce it in my head whenever I think of stage productions), I never dreamed there could be auditions for writing projects. But in the spring of 2018, I was invited by an education publisher to audition to write decodable books for beginning readers.

A decodable book is one a child can read on his or her own using word recognition, word sounds, vowel-consonant blends, and so on. The audition was to see if I would be a good fit to write these books.

Having written short stories and school textbooks for years, I thought I already was a good fit. A foolish assumption. To the editors and project directors, I was an unknown commodity. But even if I wasn't chosen for the project, I would be paid $200 for my time. Win-win.

Still, I needed this gig. Having been laid off from my part-time job at a book packager and having heard the word "No" multiple times for queried novels and other writing projects, I needed to pivot.

I was not a stranger to pivoting. Back in the 90s, when my writing hopes centered around screenwriting, I learned that Disney was offering minority screenwriters an opportunity to work in their TV division. I tried for three years, only to hear "No" every time. Glad I didn't quit my editing day job. Still, I was determined to continue writing stories even if I needed to switch to a different medium.

Auditioning for the decodable books program was a six-step process:

Step 1: Within two weeks, submit a 500-word writing sample. The sample could be something you wrote in the past.

This would be a blind submission to be vetted by the editorial team. So, there was no guarantee that my sample would be accepted.

I sent sample pages from an ESL (English as Second Language) picture book I had written for another publisher several years prior.

After anxiously waiting a whole day (not very long), I learned that I passed this part of the audition! Woo-hoo!

Step 2: If your sample is acceptable, you will be given a book premise for a grade (in this case, second grade) in order to write sample spreads.

I was assigned an editor to work with and a book concept based on a scope and sequence designed by educators. Each unit of the scope and sequence had its own word list, including words that fit a specific theme (for example, space), words the reader would already know (from past word lists in the school year or words kids learned in prior school years), and new letter combinations to work on (like words with *R-controlled* vowels like *ar* in *park*).

Step 3: In less than two weeks, write a rough draft and submit it.

After talking to the editor, who explained the company's policies for the program, I read the research articles given with the concept, and checked the word lists to make sure I was within the range of words a reader would know in order to successfully decode/read the text. This step was probably the hardest of the audition. I was new to the world of decodable books and had a learning curve. Thankfully, I had a supportive editor who walked me through the process.

Step 4: Talk to the editor for feedback.

Feedback of any kind often means a pivot. The important thing with this step was to avoid taking the feedback personally, as I unfortunately did with some past assignments. Instead, I was to do exactly what the editor suggested to produce the best book possible. The goal was for each book to eventually be adopted within a school system. Though I worked with one editor, if I was accepted as a writer for this program, anything I wrote after the audition would be reviewed by a committee dedicated to accuracy in research and in teaching the language skills.

Step 5: Make changes to and submit the sample pages within ten days.

Again, this involved a lot of rewriting before my pages were submitted.

Step 6: You will be contacted if your sample is accepted.

After anxiously waiting about five days, I learned that my sample pages were accepted. Woo-hoo! I was in!

But that was just the beginning! There were four rounds of drafts and reviews within the book-writing process.

Auditioning was one of the hardest writing experiences I've ever had. And there were more challenges to come. I had to rewrite the same book over and over and over again. When the edits came back and I had to start over, I sometimes felt like I couldn't do anything right. But there's something satisfying about taking on a hard challenge and overcoming it.

Since then, I've written seven books (which includes one dropped project) for the publisher. The process never got easier! But you know, I wouldn't have it any other way.

LINDA WASHINGTON is a curriculum editor turned freelance book editor, manuscript reviewer, and author based in Wheaton, Illinois. She has written stories and books for kids, teens, and adults. Recent projects include the picture book *Makers of the USA*, coauthored with Sandra Nickel (forthcoming, Abrams), the chapter books *Dive Day* and *Alma's Spring* (forthcoming, Great Minds) and the picture book *Esther Hobart Morris: Justice of the Peace* (Great Minds). In 2024, she wrote two chapter books currently in production for Great Minds (Dive Day and Alma's Spring). Follow her blog at https://lmarie7b.wordpress.com

The Five-Minute Talk

STACY WELLS

Several years ago, I was invited to share my journey as an author at an intensive retreat for Native writers. The invitation stirred a flood of emotions—excitement, fear, and a good dose of self-doubt. The group was a mix of established authors, emerging voices, and brand-new writers. Among them was my editor, brilliant and supportive, yes, but still, it felt like having my boss in the audience. It was daunting. My peers, my editor, all these incredible Native writers, they'd be watching me. What if I flubbed the presentation? Would my editor regret the contract? Would they kick me out of the circle?

My natural response to anything uncomfortable (especially when it's public) is usually a firm no—no risk, no uncertainty, no public displays of vulnerability. As a creative, I'm no stranger to vulnerability, but it's so much easier to do hard and uncomfortable things privately. You're the only one who knows if you fail.

However, I'd recently read *Year of Yes* by Shonda Rhimes and had resolved, like she had done, to embrace challenges. If Shonda could say yes to the unknown, surely I could say yes to a five-minute talk. By that point in my journey, I had signed with an agent and landed my first book deal. All a testament to my grit, perseverance, and a whole lot of resilience (thank you, ancestors!).

So, even as fear and imposter syndrome whispered doubts into my ear, I said yes.

With my yes firmly in place, I was ready to tackle the challenge of conveying a decade of work into five minutes. Memories poured in from the first time I sat down to write to the present moment. Each new memory played like a flipbook movie, complete with images. Emotions sprang with each flip, sharp and sweet. What could I say about my journey that would capture the countless nights of self-doubt, the quiet sacrifices, fleeting triumphs paired with the agony of rejection, but also embody the beauty of creation and the hope it inspires?

Later, I sat in a small cabin gathered around a sturdy wooden table with my fellow Native writers. My heart swelled as our conversations pivoted from discussions of favorite authors and books to a deep dive into astrological signs and back again to books, but this time stories *we* wanted to tell. Our combined presence carried an undeniable force of community and authenticity. There's a unique power when Native people gather, an energy that resonates with shared understanding and a deep sense of unity. Written history often speaks more of our erasure than our shared humanity, but here we were, becoming something greater than the sum of our parts. Like our ancestors before us who fought for our survival, we too were fighting for our existence to tell our own stories.

The people around the table, *they* were my journey.

Our "yes" to each other led me to a lifetime of people who had also said yes to me. They came to me in a linear way but also were connected to one another. People who made space for me, encouraged me, guided me, showed me possibilities, dreamt with me, opened doors, and provided opportunities. And most dearly, those who held my hand along the way. These big-hearted people made huge, pivotal impacts in my life and career.

From the strong women in my family who modeled community, to a teacher who said something so profound that she forever altered my sense of self in this huge world. From the one author who asked, "When can you come?" to another who asked, "Do you want to work with me?" The incredible mentors who gave their time and cared enough for me and my stories to speak hard truths, challenging me to grow and shaping me with their wisdom.

In that moment, I realized my journey wasn't solely defined by my perseverance and resilience. It was shaped by my community, the people who saw my potential and gave me the courage to see it too.

I survived the five-minute talk. No one booed or yawned, and my editor actually came up afterward and gave me a conversational hug. Her words of encouragement and acknowledgment were a gift I still think about to this day.

My experience taught me that there is a transformative power in saying yes to the unknown, but the greater power comes from people, both past and present. Knowing this turned my fear into gratitude and my imposter syndrome into a celebration of the connections that shaped my journey.

May you know yours, and may we be on the path of others.

*Since the original five-minute talk, I've also come to appreciate and respect the Native creatives who came before that laid the path for me to follow and allies who made sure voices like mine could be heard.

STACY WELLS *is a member of the Choctaw Nation, and a children's librarian. She is also the author of the* Tana Cooks *early chapter book series with Capstone. Her debut picture book,* Stronger Than, *co-written with Nikki Grimes and illustrated by E.B. Lewis, is forthcoming in 2026 with Heartdrum, an imprint at HarperCollins. When not reading or writing (or recommending books), she lives life to the fullest in North Texas with her family, which includes a red dog named Blu and two very adorable but very mischievous ferrets. Visit her at stacywellswrites.com.*

Your Voice, Your Story

ALICIA D. WILLIAMS

A few years ago, I had an idea for a picture book about the talk that Black and brown families give their children to keep them safe. I researched, watched YouTube and news shows, and dialogued with other parents. With pen and notebook in hand, I drafted the book as a once-upon-a-time story. It didn't work. Then, as a conversational story. That attempt failed miserably as well.

I knew this topic needed to be addressed, but the words would not come. *Perhaps*, I thought, *I was not the one to tell it*. I'm a mother of a daughter who I gave the talk to while shopping in boutiques. Who I worried about when she got her driver's license. A mother of a daughter who I fretted over with the question, *Did I prepare her enough?* Yes, I'm a concerned mother of a daughter, but not of a son.

And I'm not a man either.

So, I attempted to recruit a male poet to cowrite with. He blew me off. I proposed the idea to male peers. None took it. Finally, I let the idea go. *Whoever the idea lands with*, I said, *then so be it.*

In 2020, we all struggled with grief. We were stuck in our homes due to the pandemic. People were falling sick. Even my mom was hospitalized and was prepared to not make it home alive. Death, fear, and the unknown permeated the daily news.

Then the eight-minute video of George Floyd flooded our timelines. The video of Ahmaud Aubrey too. And the last words of Elijah McClain. I had nightmares. Insomnia. I carried a bag full worry for not only my daughter, but for my own self. *What if we're at a location and someone decides to question our presence, our simply being there?* I was traumatized over the videos of white citizens policing Black bodies for sitting, breathing, picnicking in "white spaces." What would I do? What could I do?

One night I managed a wink of sleep, and in the middle of the morning, a little voice nudged me awake. *Look at my shoes…look at my wallet…look at my friends…* The story landed back with me. It was practically written in a few hours. Yet, looking back, it was in my subconscious for several years.

This occurrence solidified four lessons for me:

One: If a story comes to you, it is yours to tell. No matter how long it takes for you to tell it. Or if you think somebody already has.

The Talk was mine to tell. Sometimes we try to limit

ourselves or claim it's too late to write the words because someone else had the same idea. But their book need not be the only one on a particular topic or with a similar storyline. There is an abundance of Christmas, first-day-of-school, Abraham Lincoln, and cooking-with-grandma books. Sometimes great minds think alike. And that's okay.

Two: Don't reject the gift of story with the excuse that it's too hard to write. I argued that I had blind spots. That I was a woman, didn't raise sons, didn't experience enough aggressions like a man.

Don't dare argue for your limitations. Writing is hard. Writing *good* stories is harder. So, my advice is to join a writer's group; continue to take classes; read read read; study study study; get a beta reader; be brave and have honest conversations. Do whatever it takes to write an authentic book.

Three: If one of those male writers had decided to accept my story idea, I would have said, *You're welcome. Glad you landed that deal.* I would have rejected the gift that was meant for me. And worse, there would have never been my take on the subject, my care for the subject, my voice wouldn't have told it.

And four, a reiteration: Even if we have the same ideas, you will write the story that you are supposed to tell. Each of us has different backgrounds, families, and traditions. We've met different people, gone to different events, made different mistakes, and learned different lessons too. We bring everything—*everything*—into our writing. We offer up scenes, characters, and dialogue that have been imbedded in us throughout our unique lives.

Here is my proof that these lessons are truth: The voice of the little boy that woke me, I knew him.

He was a little boy in the independent school where I taught. He was one of the few brown faces in his kindergarten class. Jay, as I'll call him, was routinely pulled out of class and given a talk for being too chatty, too wiggly, and too much. What kindergartener isn't?

Two years later, as I was assisting in the art classroom, his second-grade class came for their lesson. The assistant teacher of his class had the students sit on the carpet and proceeded to give Jay a talk to behave himself. I thought, *Goodness, a "bad" label has been placed on him and has followed him to second grade!*

As the art teacher began his instruction, Jay and two other students, both white, became wiggly and chatty. The art teacher stopped his lesson and told Jay to sit in a chair, while the other two were not reprimanded and were allowed to remain on the carpet. I thought, *Gosh, even the art teacher is affected by the labeling of Jay?*

Minutes later, the children got their watercolors, paper, and began to create. They were busy, giggly, and cute. They'd rise from their seats and refresh the water in their cups, and all was well. Until Jay did the same.

"Jay, what are you doing? Why aren't you in your seat?" I fussed.

Tears burst from his eyes, and he cried, "I was just getting water."

Those labels of him being a troublemaker and a bad student even reached me. I was ashamed. I was guilty, too, of not having the brave conversations with my peers regarding their biases.

So, that morning, when the little voice woke me, I was obviously given a second chance to advocate for sweet Jay.

No one would have written *The Talk* with Jay in mind or with his innocent voice. Although other writers might've experienced the same emotions, none would've held the guilt, trauma, and worries in the same manner.

So, my friends, when you write, know that books are blueprints for freedom and guide maps to escape tough realities. They will embolden and enlighten too. They will break down brick walls of fear and create flower beds of understanding and empathy. Dangerous ideas we have as writers. Dangerous because we know the potential of brilliance when readers get the right books into their hands.

Go forth, honor the story that comes to you, and tell it in the way that only you can tell it!

ALICIA D. WILLIAMS *is the award-winning author of* Genesis Begins Again, *which received the Newbery and Kirkus Prize honors, a William C. Morris finalist, and won the Coretta Scott King—John Steptoe Award for New Talent. Alicia D. also debuted a picture book biography,* Jump at the Sun: The True Life Tale of Unstoppable Storycatcher Zora Neale Hurston, *and followed up with the Jane Addams Peace Award-winning,* Shirley Chisholm Dared: The Story of the First Black Woman in Congress. *Her latest picture book,* The Talk, *won both Coretta Scott King and Golden Kite Honors. Alicia D. celebrates her verse novel,* Mid-Air, *a 2024 National Book Award longlist title.*

Alicia D. shares a passion for writing which stems from

conducting artist residencies in schools as a Master Teaching Artist of arts-integration. A graduate of the American Musical and Dramatic Academy in New York, Alicia D. infuses her love for drama, movement, comedy, and storytelling to inspire students to write their own narratives.

The Writing on the Walls

ALLAN WOLF

In 1976, when I was in the seventh grade, my writing life was launched by a single, ordinary penny.

As a poet and author of books for young people, I spend a *lot* of time in schools meeting with my readers. These children often ask me when I first knew I wanted to be a writer. In truth, one becomes a writer for a multitude of reasons that take a lifetime to truly understand. But that's not what the kids want to hear. What they *really* want to know is: *What was it specifically about my personality and my upbringing that turned me toward this writing life?* I suppose, in a way, these kids are wondering if they share any common traits or experiences—predictors that *they* might become writers as well.

I would answer, "I became a writer because I wanted

to give a voice to the voiceless." Or, "I wanted to make a difference." Or, "I wanted to let the world know that I existed by sounding 'my barbaric YAWP! to the rooftops of the world.'" Always, my answer would involve a powerful spirit inside of me, numinous and ineffable, that was writing its way out. Then, as an example, I would tell the story of how I began writing on my bedroom walls just a few weeks after turning thirteen.

Up until recently this story has been the same. I've told it so many times, in fact, that I honed it into razor-sharp focus. It goes like this:

Once upon a time, when I was in seventh grade, I was laying on my small bed in my basement bedroom in Blacksburg, Virginia, where I was raised. It was a Monday evening. A school night. The sun was already down, though even during the day, the single tiny basement window let in very little light.

For the sake of this essay, let me pause here to add a few background details that I don't typically share with the kids in my audiences. At that time in my young life, fate had recently issued me my first girlfriend *and* my first bully. I'm not sure which was the most stressful, the girlfriend or the bully, but it was a close contest. Generally speaking, I dreaded going to school. And my home was not much of a safe haven, filled as it was with the toxicity of my two older brothers' rebellion and my parents' emotionally-abusive crumbling marriage.

Let me also add that, as a kid (and my whole life) I have suffered mightily from anxiety, although back in the 1970s we didn't have that sort of helpful vocabulary. What I now recognize as anxiety was labeled cowardice in those days, or worse. Explaining this to young audiences I tend to define anxiety as the "weight of responsibility" that you may begin to feel when you move from elementary school into the upper grades.

Now back to the story.

As I lay on my bed, that Monday evening in Blacksburg, VA, I absent-mindedly flipped a penny with my thumb, watching it land on the bedspread. Heads. Tails. Heads. Etc. More likely than not, I was putting off some pressing school work. Then something unusual happened. That penny took a wild hop. It bounced off the bed and hugged the wall as it fell downward, miraculously falling into a narrow gap at the top of the wall's baseboard. The chances of me successfully making this shot on purpose would have been one in a million. The penny slid down the wall, slipped into this knife-edge-narrow gap, and, just like that, it was gone.

Well, I began to "freak out" (no doubt this had triggered a panic attack).

And at this point in my storytelling, for years, I have said the following:

It's not that I felt sorry *for the penny, but I did feel a* sense of responsibility *for letting the entire world know where the penny was! And that sense of responsibility weighed on my shoulders like a sack of potatoes.*

So instinctually I grabbed up a pencil, and right above that little opening in the baseboard I wrote this on the wall: "Penny lost down here on the night of April 12, 1976 at 2 till 9 PM and 5 seconds by Allan Dean Wolf." Immediately I felt like a million bucks. I felt light as a feather. My anxiety evaporated away. The simple act of writing down a simple fact had liberated me somehow. No more heavy sack of potatoes.

I was literally addicted. From that day forward I began writing on my bedroom walls. I wrote every day through the rest of seventh grade. And eighth grade. Through four years of high school. I gradually moved from pencils to pens to permanent markers. Somedays I would just jot a quick note. Somedays I would write non-stop for hours—not quite hypergraphia, but close. I wrote poems. I wrote nonsense. I described what I did, or what was in my head. I marked important events. I drew pictures and illustrations. I formulated mottos, declarations, and manifestos. And much of it was date-stamped, my bedroom walls becoming a 12-foot by 12-foot cubic journal of my life.

I gradually filled all four walls with words—and the entire ceiling as well. A continual tattoo of scrawling and cursing and doodling and recording and observing and lamenting and rejoicing.

I wrote deep things: "If you jumped into my soul, you would never touch bottom." I wrote confusing things: "We eat the organs of cute little bunnies." I wrote messages to my future self: "Hey Al. How did you do on tomorrow's test?" I wrote messages to my past self: "I got a C, because you never study!" And always, the content of what I wrote was never as important as the act of writing itself.

I traced my hands and wrote "I exist" on the palms. Echoes of the handprint paintings on the walls of Lascaux Cave made 17,000 years ago. Between one pair of my handprints, I drew a simple face. And suddenly it looked as if someone was on the *other* side of the wall looking inward. So, I added the words "Help! I'm trapped on the other side of this wall!" writing the letters inside-out and backwards. At the time I did it I thought it just looked cool. But now I understand that I was constructing a literal self-portrait. I was that kid living behind the wall, but writing myself into the room. I was that penny hidden behind the baseboard, writing my way out.

My parents never gave me permission, but they never stopped me. Years later my mother would tell me, "We figured if you were going to do it, it's better that you did it at home." They kept the room as is, refusing to paint over it, even though it looked as if they had raised an axe murderer in their basement. My mother would do her ironing in there. During a new HVAC installation, my father used tin snips to cut out a poem I had written (when I was twelve-years-old) on the side of a metal heating duct. He mounted and framed all three feet of it, and he sent it to me in the mail.

Even after leaving the house for college, I kept at it. I attended Virginia Tech, right there in Blacksburg. After graduation I stayed in town, working at a convenience store for a year. Then I attended Virginia Tech for two more years to earn my Master's degree. I stayed in town another year after that as a Virginia Tech instructor. All along the way, I would return to write on those walls.

When I finally moved from Virginia to Asheville, NC, I would often return home and continue writing. I began to visit with my three children who would write along with me. In total I would write on my bedroom walls for exactly forty-seven years, seven months, and sixteen days.

I have told this story for many years. I even wrote it into a fictional novel called *Zane's Trace*. I show photos to my young audiences as I talk. And up until recently, my final take-away has always been the same: I became a poet because I wanted to shout out to the world that I exist. I wanted to use my voice to declare who I am and what I stand for. Something like that.

But here is when I learned the real truth.

Recently my parents both passed away in rapid succession and my siblings and I decided we would sell the house in Blacksburg. We emptied our childhood home of every stick of furniture. We painted every inch of it a neutral white, inside and out. Every room except my bedroom. For that we had a final plan.

In a rush to complete the sale of the house by January 1, 2024, my wife and I recruited a photographer, Ken Abbott, to make a photographic record of every square inch of the walls and ceiling. And we recruited a videographer, Rod Murphy, to interview my children and my siblings about their own memories of this odd little room full of scrawl. And on December 28, 2023, we gathered in my childhood bedroom to ceremonially remove the baseboard and finally retrieve the lost penny that had set this whole thing in motion more than forty-seven years before.

Keep in mind, there were only two possible outcomes. Either the penny would be there or the penny would *not* be there. If the former, then I would be bringing the tale full-circle to a fitting conclusion. If the latter, then I had just made the whole thing up as some sort of fever dream back when I was a kid. Only two possible outcomes, right?

Well, it turns out there was a third outcome that none of us had anticipated.

With about a dozen neighbors, family, and friends all crammed into my tiny bedroom. With the camera now rolling. I discovered that I didn't even need the crowbar I had brought. The baseboard was so rotted that I was able to pull it off with my fingers. And there it was…the penny that I had lost all those years earlier. We all clapped and cheered.

But then I noticed something else.

There was actually a *second* penny hidden there as well. I held it up. I was speechless, as was everyone else in the room. How could this be? There was no way in hell that a second penny could have accidently fallen into that same tiny crack. It was my wife, Ginger West, who finally broke the silence.

She said, "You placed that second penny there yourself, so the first one wouldn't be lonely."

And she was right. In that instance it all made complete sense. As a child, I was profoundly lonely. And even though I still have no recollection of putting that second penny there, it is just the kind of thing I would have done.

And so, you see, I've been getting the story wrong all these years. The thing that *really* made me a poet. The thing that *truly* set me up to pursue this writing life, was not my desire to shout and speak and declare. It was my empathy.

For without empathy words and stories are hollow.

For years I had been joking, "It's not that I felt sorry for the penny..." And yet that's *exactly* what I had felt. And that empathy was the very spark that had set my world ablaze all those years ago.

Finally, on the evening of December 28, 2023, after nearly everyone had gone, I wrote the very last thing I would ever write on my bedroom walls. I wrote it not five feet away from the first thing I had ever written on April 12, 1976.

"Can *you* find the penny? Write yourself into existence."

Good writing has voice, volume, memorable characters, and maybe a well-wrought plot. But truly great, transcendent writing requires us to mine our own longing and connection to the world. At the core of all great writing, is empathy. That's what makes us poets.

ALLAN WOLF'S many picture books, poetry collections, and young adult novels celebrate his love of research, history, science, and poetry. He is a Los Angeles Times Book Prize finalist, two-time winner of the North Carolina Young Adult Book Award, and recipient of New York's Bankstreet College Claudia Lewis Award for Poetry. Wolf's YA novel in verse, The Watch that Ends the Night: Voices from the Titanic, was included on Booklist's 50 Best YA Books of All Time. He has three books coming in 2025, all from Candlewick Press: a poetry collection, The Gift of the Broken Teacup: Poems of Mindfulness, Meditation, and Me; a prose novel, Junius Leak and the Spiraling Vortex of Doom; and a graphic novel, The Vanishing of Lake Peigneur. Wolf lives in Asheville, NC, and Roanoke, VA. See more at www.allanwolf.com

ACKNOWLEDGMENTS

From the curator:

When I first conceived this project, I thought it would be much smaller, and that I could maybe pull off some kind of self-published project. Like the Tarot's Fool or a Labrador puppy, I bounded in, determined to make it work and yet embarrassingly naive to how much actual work—how many literal hours—it would entail. I'd already organized three anthologizes, but unlike those collections, in which I often work with contributors on two to four drafts of each story (and which take *years* from initial concept to publication), this book was different. First off, I wanted to get it done as quickly as possible—in months not years—while Hurricane Helene was still in the national consciousness. And second, I wanted to be less editor, more organizer. Thus, when asking for submissions, I explained that, unless requested, I wouldn't be giving substantial edits. My title on this project is "curator" instead of editor for that reason. After all, many of the book's contributions were previously published in other forms; they didn't need additional finessing from me. *If the pieces were handed in ready to go*, I told myself, *how much work, <u>really</u>, could it be?*

Ha.

Sometimes I amaze even myself with my naiveite. I like to think of it more as relentless optimism, but po-TAY-to, po-TAH-to. Suffice it to say, that while I *maybe* could have pulled off some kind of much smaller-scale version of this book (dogged optimist, after all!), it wouldn't resemble its current gorgeous and professional form; I would probably be even more mentally run down and exhausted than I currently find myself; and I doubt that book would have raised as much awareness and funding for Hurricane Helene relief.

What I'm trying to say is: a thousand thank yous to Sean Petrie and Burlwood Books. This collaborative project would not exist without the resources and know-how that Burlwood provided, along with the tireless efforts of Burlwood's staff. Huge props also to creative designer Andrea Wofford, copyeditor Eli Karren, and marketing director Natalie Runnels. Burlwood is a small professional press that does HUGE work. Please check them out at www.burlwoodbooks.com.

This project also would not exist without the generous contributors who donated their creative work. Thank you all, not only for saying yes, but for doing so enthusiastically and emphatically. The turnaround on this project was lightning-fast for the publishing world, and you all stepped up, in some cases putting paying projects on hold until you sent in your contribution. I am forever grateful.

Special thanks to contributors Lockie Hunter, Constance Lombardo, and Linda-Marie Barrett for volunteering to coordinate Asheville reading events to help get out the word. Taking this off my plate gave me more time to grieve and process the loss of my dad with my family. Thank you.

Extra special thanks to Asheville artist Kelsey Lecky, who *spent over 100 hours in a week and a half* creating an incredible 12x18 inch, stained glass piece, which will be auctioned off and proceeds donated to *Beloved Asheville* and *World Central Kitchen*. Kelsey's art is featured in its entirety on the back cover so it can be viewed without text obstruction. It will also be the front cover of the audio version of *Spinning Toward the Sun*, which is forthcoming. Although Kelsey's business was severely impacted during Helene, she nonetheless donated to this project. Please consider checking out www.kakleckyillustration.com for prints, original art, and commissions.

Thank you to my ever-supportive family: my partner, three kids, my sister, and momma. Thanks to my late father, for gifting me with storytelling and ferocious stubbornness *cough*— I mean—tenacity. Whatever you call it, it's helpful in the publishing world.

One last note, about the power of authentic community and connection, in case you're reading this and thinking you could never do something like this. I met Sean in my very first writing workshop in graduate school. He wrote one of my favorite submissions (still waiting for you to get back to and sub that middle grade adventure novel, Sean). Anyway, Sean was a year ahead of me in school, so we didn't actually become close friends until a few years later when, before either of us were published, we served as graduate assistants together. But here's the thing. During that first workshop (in which I was terrified, had oh-so-much-to-learn, and yes I did go directly to my dorm after workshop and cry in the shower, but never mind) Sean was kind. No one was mean, exactly, but Sean clarified and reframed some comments people made about my work in ways that terrified-first-semester Nora could handle. He might not even remember that workshop, but I do. I will forever. And his original kindness made it much more likely that we would become friends, and later work together.

My point is that how you treat people and how you interact with them at every stage in life really matters. Sean wasn't a published author or editor at that time, and he certainly didn't own a publishing company back then. And I wasn't published, nor did I ever imagine I'd one day become an anthologist. We were both just creatives who cared about other people. Who became friends. Who grew in our careers and eventually teamed up to create this book. That's how stuff like this book—really cool stuff—happens. And no matter what kind of creative you are, there's no reason you can't do it, too.

Thanks for reading. Now go be nice, make a new friend, and create art. All of us doing those things, that's how we'll change the world.

-- Nora Shalaway Carpenter

From the publisher:

A repeated huge thank you to **Kelsey Lecky,** for the stunning stained glass art that she created just for this book. If only it were possible to capture its sunshine-y brilliance in print! But the back cover, featuring it like a framed work of art, comes darn close. Thanks for your time and artistic genius, Kelsey!

And speaking of the cover, endless gratitude to **Andrea Wofford**, our wizard of design. This book simply wouldn't be the same without your amazing talent. Thank you for adjusting to our repeated tweaks and being able to pivot when we needed it most. Heck yes we can judge this book by its cover!

We can also judge it by its meticulously copy-edited interior, thanks to eagle-eye **Eli Karren**. Endless gratitude for your time and attention to detail. Thanks for keeping us MLA-compliant and error-free! (Any typos that remain are all mine.)

Are you holding this book in your hands? Or maybe reading the e-book on a screen? Chances are, that's because of the wide-reaching efforts of our marketing guru, **Natalie Runnels**. Thank you again and again, Natalie, for being there with idea after idea, a brilliant spreadsheet (no easy feat!), and your enthusiasm and skill in making this book quite literally get seen by so many. We need a press release to celebrate *you!*

Lastly, this book, of course, would never have happened without the amazing, generous, and just all-around wonderful person and good friend, **Nora Shalaway Carpenter**. Life throws so much at us, right? And there you are, still standing tall and moving forward, doing things, doing *something,* anything. Whether a kind word or putting together an entire book. I'm so proud to be part of this project, and even more so to call you friend. The world needs more people like you, if we're going to make it through these times.

And the world needs more people like **all the authors who've contributed to this book.** Who've not just contributed—who have donated their time and words and skill to this book. I've been honored to work with you. Here's hoping these pages find the readers who need them most.

-- Sean Petrie

ESSAY CREDITS

- Huda Al-Marashi, *The Dictator in My Notebook*. An earlier version of this essay first appeared in the *VIDA Review* in April 2017.

- Tanya Aydelott, *An Invitation to the Party*. A version of this essay appeared in the Nerdy Book Club blog in April 2019.

- Chris Barton, *Remembering Our Worst Times, and Making the Most of Them*. This essay first appeared in a *School Library Journal* post on March 24, 2020, at https://www.slj.com/story/chris-barton-all-of-a-sudden-forever-nonfiction-childrens-tough-topics

- Nora Shalaway Carpenter, *An Antidote to Fear*. This essay is adapted from a talk given during the first meeting of The Rural Assembly of English Language and Literacy Education (TRAELLE) at the 2024 National Council of the Teachers of English annual conference.

- Cinda Williams Chima, *Imposter Syndrome and the Value of the Day Job.* This essay is adapted from the author's previous Substack posts.

- Rob Costello, *Hold Onto Your (Writer) Friends in Dark Times.* An alternate version of this essay appeared in the R(ev)ise and Shine! Substack newsletter on October 15, 2024.

- Lockie Hunter, *Room for Purple Horses: An Exploration in Finding Authentic Voice.* This essay first appeared in a similar form in *Hip Mama Magazine* #38, The Labor Issue, September 2007.

- Jennifer Richard Jacobson, *Motivation and Swim Buddies.* This essay originally appeared in the R(ev)ise and Shine! Substack newsletter on May 15, 2024.

- Lyn Miller-Lachmann, *Giving Characters Agency in Restricted Situations.* This piece is based on two essays that appeared on the author's blog, at https://lynmillerlachmann.com/category/blog/.

- Gloria Muñoz, *What Climate Fiction Can Teach Us About Hope.* This essay first appeared in an *SLJ Teen Librarian Toolbox* post on January 8, 2025, at https://teenlibrariantoolbox.com/2025/01/08/what-climate-fiction-can-teach-us-about-hope-a-guest-post-by-gloria-munoz/

- Beth Revis, *Layering in the Details That Matter.* Some elements of this essay first appeared in the author's Patreon materials.

- Jess Rinker, *How I Survive a Monolithic Life*. A version of this essay first appeared in an *SLJ Teen Librarian Toolbox* post on January 12, 2024, at https://teenlibrariantoolbox.com/2024/01/12/how-to-be-okay-when-life-feels-monolithic-a-guest-post-by-jess-rinker/

- Liz Garton Scanlon, *Responding to the Unknown: Creativity as Both Answer and Inspiration*. Variations of this essay were presented by the author as lectures at SCBWI-Asilomar and at the Mazza Museum.

- Lindsey Stoddard, *What We Carry in Our Guts*. This essay first appeared in an *SLJ Teen Librarian Toolbox* post on October 21, 2022, located at https://teenlibrariantoolbox.com/2022/10/21/a-guest-post-by-lindsey-stoddard/

- Meera Trehan, *Becoming a Writer*. A version of this essay was published in the Winter/Spring 2022 issue of *The Writer's Center Magazine*.

- Padma Venkatraman, *Body Language: Acting Out, Scenes Without Obscene Gestures, and Other Effective Ways to Show Emotion*. This essay was first published in the Society of Children's Book Writers and Illustrators' Bulletin.

- Alexandra Villasante, *Inside Out: Creating Voice Through Building Your Character*. This essay is based on a workshop the author taught at the Highlights Foundation.

ABOUT THE NONPROFITS

All proceeds from *Spinning Toward the Sun* will be donated to **Beloved Asheville** and **World Central Kitchen**, two nonprofit groups who were and continue to be lifesaving resources for victims of Hurricane Helene.

Beloved Asheville is a grassroots, equity-focused organization in Asheville, North Carolina, with an incredible record of service. It was one of the first organizations to get boots on the ground when Hurricane Helene decimated much of Asheville and the surrounding towns, and is still helping the years-long recovery. To learn more, please visit www.BelovedAsheville.com

World Central Kitchen has a similar record of service, although this larger organization is also able to respond to disasters worldwide. Just like Beloved Asheville, its recovery aid to Helene victims was almost immediate: by quickly teaming with local volunteer chefs, it provided hundreds of thousands of gallons of drinking water and hot, fresh meals to families and individuals in need, and is still offering much-needed relief. Learn more at www.wck.org/relief/hurricane-helene

ABOUT BURLWOOD

Burlwood Books is a small, independent press in Austin, Texas, that began as a favor to a grieving family, and grew into even more.

We strive to publish books that others may overlook. Our pages are full of unapologetically-accessible poems and paint-splatted art. Of proudly diverse voices. Of debut authors and established writers. Of swirling stories, just waiting for the right person to look inside.

We hope you enjoy the beauty in the burl.

To learn more, please visit www.BurlwoodBooks.com

Our Story

A discussion with Burlwood founder Sean Petrie

Q: How did Burlwood Books come about?

Burlwood arose as a favor to a grieving family. (Trigger warning: domestic violence in this paragraph.) In 2022, I met 26-year-old Austin poet Erika Evans, when she was typing poems for strangers in front of a restaurant in my neighborhood. I'm part of Typewriter Rodeo, a group of poets who also type poems for strangers, so I would often stop and chat with Erika. She had a great energy and such an easy, engaging way with people, so I asked if she wanted to join a Typewriter Rodeo event. Her eyes lit up: "Oh my goodness yes!" But when the event came, she never showed. A few days later I learned she was murdered while on a trip with an abusive male companion.

Erika's family held a memorial in front of the restaurant where she typed. At the memorial, I wrote a poem in her honor and placed it in the tribute book. Later, Erika's dad reached out to give me Erika's typewriter, for our group to use in her honor. "Erika created so many beautiful poems and paintings," he told me. "I wish I knew how to share them."

I had no idea how I would do it, but I offered to put together a book of Erika's poetry and art for her family. Because Erika's death had made the national news, a designer in Portland, Oregon, donated her time to do the cover.

And a few months later, I shared that book, called *Allowing for Time,* with Erika's family. They then asked to share it with the world, so I formed Burlwood Books to do that, to make Erika's book available worldwide.

All of its proceeds go to victims of domestic violence.

Q: Why the name Burlwood?

It's a pretty great term for being beautifully different.

A burl is a part of a tree that is considered an "abnormal" growth—usually a big lumpy protrusion somewhere along the trunk. But on the inside it's gorgeous—the woodgrain is all swirled and bent, and burlwood is often prized for use in craft furniture or decorative art. I love that idea—that, on the outside, a burl is something people wouldn't think of as beautiful, and actually think the opposite because it looks different from the rest of the tree. But if you take the time to look inside, it's uniquely breathtaking. That's what I hope our books are like. We take manuscripts that traditional publishers might think are too different for their tastes, and we celebrate those differences and whorls and whimsy.

Q: What made you expand past that first book?

I didn't intend for Burlwood to publish more books. But it took on a life of its own. Soon after I'd published *Allowing for Time*, a poet with Typewriter Rodeo, LaCole Foots, told me she'd written a poetry collection and was looking for a publisher. I loved LaCole's poems, and so I said, "Well, I kinda know how to do that now. And I have a publishing company already set up." LaCole was thrilled at the idea of publishing with Burlwood, I hired a cover designer and copyeditor, and *Heavy Light* was born.

The same year, another Rodeo poet, Rebecca Bendheim, showed me her collection of poems about her coming out journey. I loved those and, with multiple books under the Burlwood belt, offered to publish them. And so we were able to share *Coming Out Party*—Rebecca's poems paired with Sarah Rosa Glickman's heartfelt art—with the world.

Q: What does it mean for you to publish diverse voices?
Diversity is reality. Books should reflect it, not fear it.

For the most part, traditional and mainstream U.S. publishers have focused on books from the perspective of the majority—whether race, gender, ethnicity, religion, or simply who to love. That's like only telling the story of oaks and elms. There are a hundred thousand other species of trees in the forest. Burlwood celebrates the value of that diversity. That's why we're more than proud to publish books from a variety of voices. We choose to see the beauty in the burl, and the beauty in the world—*all* of it.

On a broader level, our country's history is replete with laws that have oppressed minority voices. As President Trump's Department of Education stated in February 2025: "Segregation was a shameful darker period in our country's history." And segregation is just one example—throughout history, our laws forced minority groups to bear unique moral and financial burdens. To name just a few: not being allowed to own property (while majority groups passed theirs down through generations); being stripped of property through manifest destiny, internment camps, and slavery; redlining; grandfather clauses; not being able to vote; not being able to marry; not being able to have individual banking accounts. Many of those laws persisted to the 1980s. Some still do. Burlwood chooses to acknowledge our country's history head-on, rather than pretending it didn't happen. Hiding from history is just another form of oppression.

Q: How would you describe Burlwood's mission?
Burlwood Books is committed to helping books exist in a world where they might not otherwise get seen.

Spinning Toward the Sun is also available as an e-book and an audio book.

Made in United States
Troutdale, OR
04/02/2025